Grape
Expeditions
in
California

A wine bottle fits perfectly into your downtube-mounted bottle cage. Hardly Consumer Products Safety Commission-approved, but it works.

You can ride or drive these tours!

If you're going to drink a lot, bring a friend.

Grape Expeditions in California

15 Tours across the California Wine Country

5th Edition

by Lena Emmery & Sally Taylor
Maps by Sheldon Greenberg
Composition by Helen Epperson
Marginal Rider by David Robinson, Words & Art (HK)

If you don't have a sense of humor, don't buy this book.

ISBN 0-934101-00-0

 This is a tailor-made book.

Published by
Sally Taylor & Friends
1442 Willard Street
San Francisco CA 94117 USA
(415) 824-1563

Printed in Hong Kong by
Professional Printers, Ltd.

ISBN 0-934101-00-0

ON THE COVER: Dehlinger Vineyards in Sonoma County. Photo by the authors. Bike compliments of Velo City, 638 Stanyan St., San Francisco 94117.

"We invite you to take a bicycle tour of the wine country, to discover the land's most pleasant harvest."

Wear a helmet—safety knows no season.

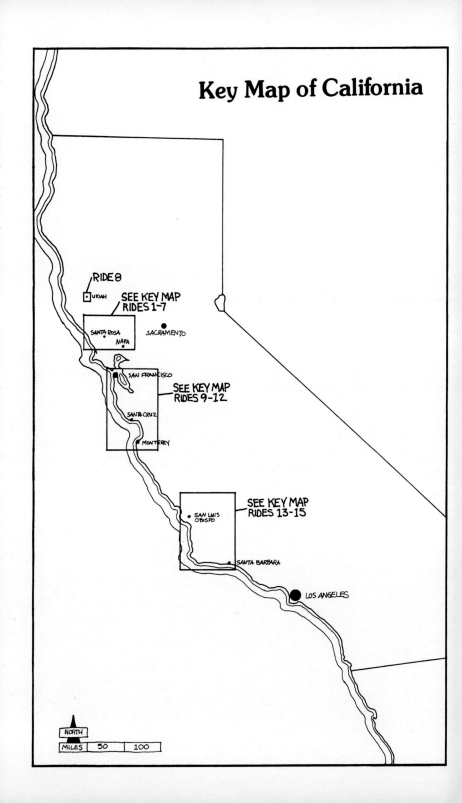

Table of Contents

Preliminaries

This fifth edition of *Grape Expeditions* includes some new routes and many new wineries (99 in all) in the constantly evolving California wine country.

Many of the wineries are small, owner-operated enterprises, so be prepared to adjust your visit to the work schedules of the winemaker. Please try to make reservations at least a day or two in advance wherever we have indicated "by appointment"; your courtesy will be well rewarded. Most of the wineries are open from 10 to 4; we have noted the exceptions. We suggest you keep your group small; the wineries and the roads will deal with you more kindly.

We've included a wide array of accommodations, from campgrounds to deluxe bed and breakfast establishments, and reservations are suggested. Our "Selected Stops" and the wineries we have chosen are but a sampling of what the wine country has to offer; we encourage you to make your own special discoveries.

Our format allows you to custom-"Taylor" your ride to suit your time, interests, and endurance. See the alternate routes. You can also connect several rides (connect the dots) for a weekend or a week of exploring. Be sure to carry water or ERG, since summer temperatures can pass 90 degrees. Winter will be a pleasant 40 to 70 degrees. Winds generally prevail from the north and are much stronger in the afternoon.

Weekends in summer the roads are crowded, so wear a helmet for protection and for visibility. The length and relative difficulty of the rides are described at the beginning of each chapter. Most are neither long nor hard, but note, several are not for marginal riders.

Gear ratios are for a multigeared lightweight cycle; mileages are approximate.

We make every attempt to have accurate up-to-date information. If you find an error, your letter to us will earn you a free copy of the next edition.

Now pump up those tires and enjoy yourself!!

Lena Emmery & Sally Taylor
San Francisco
July 1987

The North Coast
Tours 1 – 8

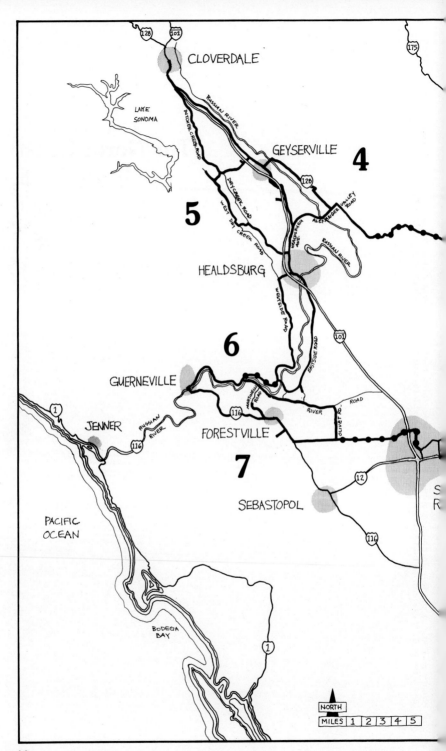

Tours 1 – 7

Connect the dots for a week's tour

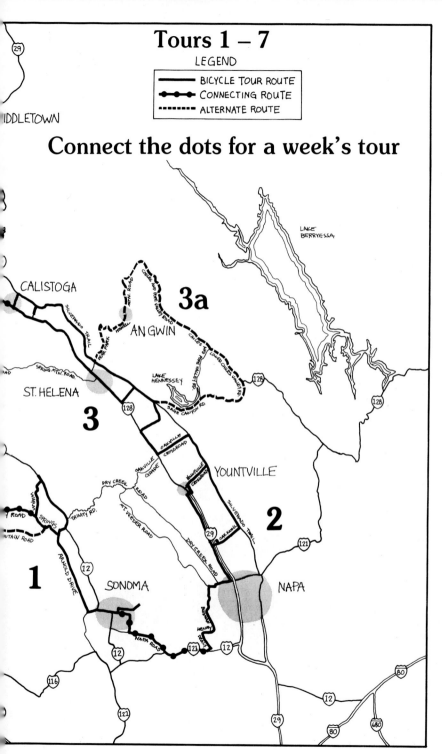

Courtesy: Kenwood Vineyards

Stop at Morton's Warm Springs for a swim in the pear-shaped pool, on the left-hand side of Warm Springs Road. There's a bike rack in the parking lot.

Sonoma Valley 1

CYCLING THE VALLEY OF THE MOON

Distance: 23 miles, with a 15-mile alternate route.
Terrain: Flat, except the alternate route. Gearing in the 40s.

Starting in the old town of Sonoma, park anywhere, and stock up on picnic supplies at the Sonoma Cheese Factory, the Sonoma French Bakery, or any of the other tasty places on the square that suit your fancy.

SEBASTIANI The winery, tasting room, and residences of this Sonoma family operation are tucked back on Fourth Street East, just 3 blocks from the town square. Now one of the largest wineries in the county, this one is still family-run, with lots of regional memorabilia.

BUENA VISTA Continuing north on Fourth Street East, the road turns right, shortly, as it becomes Lovall Valley Road. Stay on Lovall Valley, or watch for the bike route signs, for less than a mile, then turn left onto Old Winery Road, where the signs to Buena Vista Winery will lead you to the oldest winery in the North Coast (now owned by a German firm). Nestled among tall oak and eucalyptus, the old stone winery is a cool respite. In summer, on weekends, they have outdoor classical music concerts here.

On the way back to the square, stop on Second Street East at the Vella Cheese Company. They make their own excellent cheeses, and the prices are as basic as their retail counter. No frills, just great cheese.

Cross the square, heading west, on West Napa Street; bear left when you intersect Highway 12 and continue on Petaluma Avenue. At Arnold Drive, turn right, heading north up the Valley of the Moon to Glen Ellen. This sleepy town remains famous for its famous resident, Jack London. Read his book, *The Valley of the Moon,* to find out why.

GLEN ELLEN WINERY A short climb up London Ranch Road will bring you to this energetic family winery, run by the Benzigers.

If you don't want to climb, just continue through Glen Ellen on Arnold. Turn left at Dunbar Road, just before Arnold ends at Highway 12.

GRAND CRU Follow Dunbar to Henno Road. Turn left and then, shortly, left again on Vintage Lane. There, just behind the Dunbar School, is this small winery, specializing in German-style wines, including some "botrytised" wines which you should taste, if you never have before. The "noble rot" of France and Germany gives a distinctive honey character to the California wines, too.

13

You're in the Valley of the Moon—but please—confine your riding to daylight hours.

Dunbar Road ends at Highway 12, which you'll have to endure 2 miles to the town of Kenwood. Watch the traffic.

KENWOOD Out of the old Italian tradition, Kenwood Vineyards, just a short distance north of town on Highway 12, was once just a big barn full of redwood barrels. Now it's polished stainless steel. Still, the warm friendliness of the Lee family pervades the tasting room. Their reds, Zinfandels and Cabernet, still have that Italian robustness, and their whites are very sophisticated.

CHATEAU ST. JEAN Still at the helm of this 1970s winery, winemaker Dick Arrowood guards the excellent whites with a Teutonic dedication. But the operation now belongs to Suntory, of Japan. The garden surrounding the old Goff mansion is great for picnics. Before heading back, if you still haven't tired of tasting, try the St. Francis Winery, right on Highway 12.

Alternate Route

MATANZAS CREEK The alternate route, a 15-mile, hilly ride up Warm Springs Road to Matanzas Creek Winery, gets even more challenging after you stop at the winery (where you'll need an appointment), if you return to Glen Ellen via Sonoma Mountain Road. Traffic will be no problem, but two steep climbs, and plenty of potholes on the downhill parts, make this alternate strictly for experienced cyclists.

WINERIES TO VISIT

Buena Vista Winery, 18000 Old Winery Road, Sonoma 95476. (707) 938-1266. Open daily.

Chateau St. Jean, 8555 Sonoma Hwy. 12, Kenwood 95452. (707) 833-4134. Open daily 10–4:30.

Glen Ellen Winery, 1883 London Ranch Road, Glen Ellen 95442. (707) 996-1066. Open daily.

Grand Cru Vineyards, 1 Vintage Lane, Glen Ellen 95442. (707) 996-8100. Open daily.

Kenwood Vineyards, 9592 Sonoma Hwy. 12, Kenwood 95452. (707) 833-5891. Open daily.

Matanzas Creek Winery, 6097 Bennett Valley Road, Santa Rosa 95404. (707) 528-6464. By appointment only.

Sebastiani Vineyards, 389 Fourth St. East, Sonoma 95476. (707) 938-5532. Open daily.

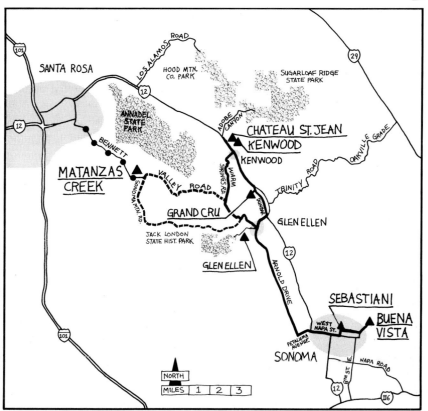

SELECTED STOPS

Morton's Warm Springs, 1651 Warm Springs Road, Kenwood 95452. (707) 833-5511. Open May 15 to Labor Day.

Sonoma Cheese Factory, 2 Spain St., Sonoma 95476. (707) 938-5225.

Sonoma French Bakery, 468 First St. East, Sonoma 95476. (707) 996-2691. Open Wed–Sat, 9–6; Sun, 7:30–12.

Vella Cheese Co., 315 Second St. East, Sonoma 95476. (707) 938-3232.

Sugarloaf Ridge State Park (campgrounds), 2 miles NE of Kenwood via Adobe Canyon Road. (707) 833-5712. Primitive sites.

London Lodge, Glen Ellen 95442. (707) 938-8510.

Thistle Dew Inn, 171 W. Spain St., Sonoma 95476. (707) 938-2909.

Bed & Breakfast hotline: Inns of Sonoma, PO Box 51, Geyserville 95441. (707) 433-INNS.

BICYCLE ASSISTANCE: Sonoma Wheels, 523 Broadway, Sonoma 95476. (707) 935-1366.

2 Sonoma to Yountville

ANOTHER VALLEY OF OLD WINERIES

Distance: 19 miles
Terrain: Nearly flat, but windy afternoons are almost guaranteed, from the northwest. Gearing in the 50s should suffice.

> **To Connect with Ride 1.**
>
> Starting in Sonoma, at the Square, follow East Napa Street (which turns into South Napa Street) and turn right at Eighth Street, just before the railroad tracks. Follow Eighth down to Napa Road. Turn left there, and in 2½ miles the road runs right into Highway 121. Turn left here and take care: the road is narrow and the cars are fast. Go 3 miles to Mont St. John Cellars.

MONT ST. JOHN Start in the parking lot of this winery, at the junction of Old Sonoma Road and Highway 121. This is the Carneros district of Napa Valley, where a lot of people hope to make the perfect Pinot Noir, the grape from which the great Burgundies are made. Take Old Sonoma Road towards Napa, and turn left at Dealy Lane.

CARNEROS CREEK Tucked away in the vineyards, a mile up Dealy Lane, is a small friendly winery open for tours, by appointment, but the salesroom is open weekdays.

From here, continue on the quiet back roads skirting downtown Napa. Dealy Lane ends at Henry Road. Turn right here and continue to Buhman Avenue. Turn left onto Buhman which ends at Browns Valley. Turn left again. Browns Valley swings to the right and ends at Redwood Road. Turn right, now, and head towards Napa. Before you reach Highway 29, at a light about 1 mile down, turn left onto Solano Avenue, a designated bike path. Heading north, now, up the Napa Valley, in two miles cross Highway 29 on Oak Knoll Avenue. Watch the railroad tracks.

16

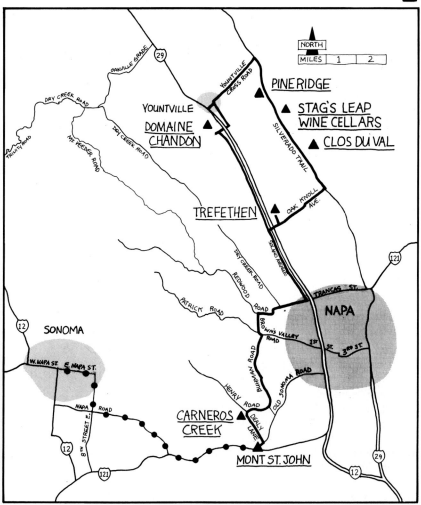

North

MILES 1 2

OAKVILLE GRADE

29

PINERIDGE ▲

▲ **STAG'S LEAP WINE CELLARS**

DRY CREEK ROAD

YOUNTVILLE CROSS ROAD

YOUNTVILLE

DOMAINE CHANDON ▲

▲ **CLOS DU VAL**

TRINITY ROAD

MT. VEEDER ROAD

DRY CREEK ROAD

SILVERADO TRAIL

TREFETHEN ▲

OAK KNOLL AVE.

121

SOLANO AVENUE

DRY CREEK ROAD

REDWOOD ROAD

PATRICK ROAD

TRANCAS ST.

NAPA

12

SONOMA

W. NAPA ST. E. NAPA ST.

BROWN'S VALLEY ROAD

1ST ST. 3RD ST.

BUHMAN ROAD

NAPA ROAD

HENRY ROAD

DEALY LANE

OLD SONOMA ROAD

8TH STREET E.

CARNEROS CREEK ▲

12

121

MONT ST. JOHN ▲

12

29

Alternate Start

This tour can be taken in reverse, starting from Vintage 1870.

TREFETHEN   Just 100 yards on the left is the long driveway to a fine winery over 100 years old, now run by John and Janet Trefethen. All the wine is made from the family vineyards, and awards abound.

Returning to Oak Knoll Avenue, turn left, leaving the winery and continue on this quiet road to the Silverado Trail. Turn left here and enjoy the wide-shouldered alternate route up the Napa Valley, a cyclist's delight.

CLOS DU VAL   The next winery, a mile up the road on the right, is owned by an American and run by a Frenchman. Their efforts blend both worlds of wine, and their artist-of-choice is Ronald Searle. His wonderful, wacky cartoons, often used in winery promotions, are to the world of wine what our Marginal Rider is to this book.

STAG'S LEAP WINE CELLARS   Another mile up the Silverado Trail, again on the right, this winery makes great Cabernet. Winemaker Warren Winiarski stumped a panel of French wine experts in 1977. They thought it was a fine Bordeaux. The retail shop and picnic grounds are available, but there is no tasting.

PINE RIDGE   Continue up the Trail another ¼ mile on the other side of the road. This relatively new winery has both picnic and tasting facilities.

Go one last mile up the Trail to the Yountville Crossroads, passing Silverado Winery, up on a knoll, the latest venture of the Disney family, but not open to the public. The Crossroad shoots left across the valley to Yountville, now a collection of restaurants, antique stores, and little bed & breakfast places centered around Vintage 1870, an old winery turned into a complex of "shoppes."
In the back of Vintage 1870 is Groezinger's, one of the best wine shops in the Valley. The Court of the Two Sisters Bakery, next door, should be avoided if you don't like French pastry.

DOMAINE CHANDON   Cross Highway 29 just south of Yountville, on the way to the Veterans' Home, to find out what the French Champagne house of Moet & Chandon could do in the New World. Built in 1976, the winery specializes in sparkling wine, gives a great tour of its very modern complex, and features a fabulous restaurant. Everything is first class, maybe too formal for a tired and sweaty cyclist. Make reservations in advance.

Lodging in Yountville is very cozy and pricey. Camping at the Bothe–Napa State Park is 15 miles north, beyond St. Helena (Tour 3), or try the B&B referral number.

By appointment only. Use your bicycle cellular phone.

Opening a Bottle of Sparkling Wine

Place napkin or towel over bottle. Remove wire hood. Try not to damage lower portion of metal foil.

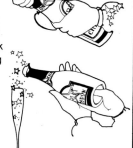

Grasp the cork (still covered with napkin). Tilt bottle away from you and other people. Hold the cork and turn the bottle, letting the cork ease out.

A thumb in the punt will give added control when pouring.

WINERIES TO VISIT

Carneros Creek, 1285 Dealy Lane, Napa 94558. (707) 253-9463. Tours by appointment only.

Clos Du Val, 5330 Silverado Trail, Napa 94558. (707) 252-6711. Open daily.

Domaine Chandon, California Drive, Yountville 94599. (707) 944-2280. Closed Mon–Tues from Nov–Apr. Restaurant reservations: (707) 944-2892.

Mont St. John Cellars, 5400 Old Sonoma Road, Napa 94558. (707) 255-8864. Open daily.

Pine Ridge, 5901 Silverado Trail, Napa 94558. (707) 253-7500. Closed Monday.

Stag's Leap Wine Cellars, 5766 Silverado Trail, Napa 94558. (707) 944-2020. Retail sales. Tours by appointment.

Trefethen Vineyards, 1160 Oak Knoll Ave., Napa 94558. (707) 255-7700. Closed Sunday.

SELECTED STOPS

Vintage 1870, 6525 Washington, Yountville 94599. Open 10–5:30 daily.

Best Western Napa Valley Lodge, Madison Ave., Yountville 94599. (707) 944-2468. Rental bikes available.

Bed & Breakfast Referral, Carol Knight, 1834 First St., Napa 94558. (707) 257-1051.

Bothe–Napa Valley State Park, 3801 St. Helena Hwy. North, Calistoga 94515. (707) 942-4575. Complete facilities for cyclists.

BICYCLE ASSISTANCE: The Bicycle Works, 3335 Solano Ave., Napa 94558. (707) 253-7000.

Bryan's Napa Valley Cyclery, 4088 Byway East (at Information Center tower), Napa 94558. (707) 255-3377. Open daily.

3 The Napa Valley

HAPPY TRAILS TO YOU

Distance: 40 miles, round trip.
Terrain: Gentle rolling hills. Winds from the northwest. Gearing in the 50s.

Starting in Yountville, take the Yountville Crossroads across the valley to the Silverado Trail. Turn left there and, 1 mile later, left again at the Oakville Crossroads.

You are now heading toward Highway 29. We avoid Highway 29 as much as possible, though there are plenty of good wineries along that route; there's just too much traffic and too many railroad tracks.

SILVER OAK CELLARS About a mile down the Crossroads on the left is the site of the old Oakville Dairy, now a winery run by Justin Meyer, a Napa Valley personality.

At Highway 29, the Oakville Grocery, on the corner, has gourmet picnic supplies. Pometta's Deli is a short way south, across the highway, on the Oakville Grade Road, with roast chicken, artichoke hearts and malfatti, the naked Napa Valley ravioli.

ROBERT MONDAVI WINERY At Oakville, turn right up Highway 29 for a short distance to one of the best winery tours and biggest winery success stories in the recent history of the valley. The elegant archway is visible on the left. Cross the road carefully; watch the railroad tracks. Robert Mondavi and his family are innovators in everything from winery architecture to barrel aging. Take the tour if it's not too busy.

Continue on Highway 29 north towards Rutherford.

PEJU PROVINCE On the way, a new winery, on the right, welcomes cyclists with Cabernet, Sauvignon Blanc and Chardonnay made in the tradition of Provence, France, where the Romans introduced enology 2,000 years ago. Anthony Peju is in charge.

At Rutherford, cross back over to the preferred route, the Silverado Trail. You might want to stop here to visit Inglenook and Beaulieu, two of the valley's biggest wineries, now owned by the British firm, Grand Met. There is a deli in Rutherford Square.

The Rutherford Crossroads doglegs across the valley to the Trail. Take the left at Caymus Vineyards (a fine old family winery) and at the stop sign you have a number of choices.

Alternate Route

Turn right on the Silverado Trail from the Rutherford Crossroads. It's a short jog to Sage Canyon Road, on the left, and the challenging alternate route (see Ride 3a).

Softies should turn left, or stop here for a tasting.

CONN CREEK Just at the corner, another fine Napa Valley winery offers tastings, at $1.25 a glass. You might prefer to hurry on, as this wide-shouldered stretch of road north to Calistoga is wine country cycling at its best.

NAPA CREEK WINERY About a mile up, on the left, is a young, energetic winery, with free tastings and informal tours, and which welcomes cyclists.

CUVAISON The next five miles are for cycling, and include one short uphill pull. Look to the right, after the descent, for a tasting room, with picnic tables out front. Owned by the Swiss family, Schmidheiny, this winery features excellent Chardonnay, Cabernet and Zinfandel, in small quantities. They also have great T-shirts.

It's just a country mile up Silverado Trail to Calistoga. Turn left at the T, to short-cut through town, or make a loop around the back of town and see the old geysers, by turning right at the T and then left onto Tubbs Lane.

CHATEAU MONTELENA This is another worthy stop, and includes a Japanese garden as well as white wines that fooled the French at the same time Stags Leap reds did. (See Ride 2.)

Continue on Tubbs to Highway 29 and turn left, south, back to Calistoga, and on towards St. Helena. If you stop for the natural springs and mud baths in Calistoga, plan to spend the night! There are plenty of old-style hotels and great restaurants.

STERLING VINEYARDS Just a mile south of town, up on the hill to the left, is this Greek monastery-style facility now owned by Seagram of Canada. Enter on Dunaweal and leave your bike at the parking lot at the bottom, taking the tram to get the tour, tasting and view.

Continue south on Highway 29 towards St. Helena, passing both Bothe–Napa Valley State Park and the Bale Grist Mill on the right. This is a wider, quieter road than 29 becomes, south of St. Helena. Stop as often as you like, but plan to cross over to the Silverado Trail, sooner, not later.

MARKHAM About 4 miles down on the left, this family-run, estate-bottled winery offers contrast to the imposing Christian Brothers stone edifice a little farther down on the right. It was recently reopened and is worth a visit. So is the Rhine House of Beringer (now owned by the Swiss firm, Nestle). But these biggest establishments tend to be overcrowded.

RAYMOND Just south of St. Helena, if you haven't turned over to the Silverado Trail already, turn left at Zinfandel Lane, stopping for a taste at this winery run by the great-grandchildren of Jacob Beringer. Then continue to the Silverado Trail and back to Yountville, where you started.

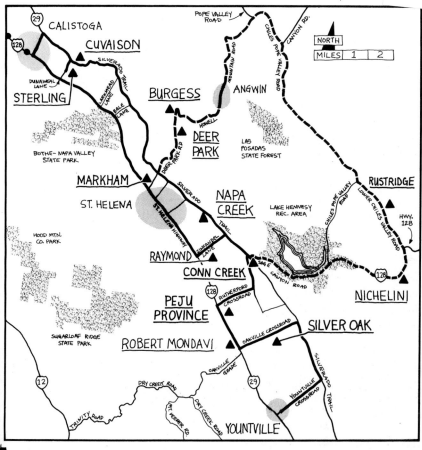

Cross railroad tracks at right angles.

WINERIES TO VISIT

Conn Creek, 8711 Silverado Trail, St. Helena 94574. (707) 963-9100. Open 11–4 on weekends, 1–4 weekdays. $1.25/glass for tasting.

Cuvaison Winery, 4550 Silverado Trail, Calistoga 94515. (707) 942-6266. Open daily.

Markham Winery, 2812 North St. Helena Hwy. (29), St. Helena 94574. (707) 963-5292. Open daily.

Robert Mondavi Winery, 7801 St. Helena Hwy. (29), Oakville 94562. (707) 963-9611. Tasting with tour only.

Napa Creek Winery, 1001 Silverado Trail, St. Helena 94574. (707) 963-9456. Open daily.

Peju Province, 8466 St. Helena Hwy. (29), Rutherford 94573. (707) 963-3600. Open daily, 10–6.

Raymond Vineyard & Cellar, 849 Zinfandel Lane, St. Helena 94574. (707) 963-3141.

Silver Oak Cellars, 915 Oakville Crossroad, Oakville 94562. (707) 944-8808.

Sterling Vineyards, 1111 Dunaweal Lane, Calistoga 94515. (707) 942-5141. Open daily, 10:30–4:30. Tram $5, with $2 discount on first bottle purchased.

SELECTED STOPS

Calistoga Inn, 1250 Lincoln Ave., Calistoga 94515. (707) 942-4101.

Bed & Breakfast Exchange, 1458 Lincoln Ave., #3, Calistoga 94515. (707) 942-5900.

Bothe–Napa Valley State Park. Campsites. (See Ride 2.)

Dr. Wilkerson's Hot Springs, 1507 Lincoln Ave., Calistoga 94515. (707) 942-4102. Mud baths.

BICYCLE ASSISTANCE: St. Helena Cyclery, 1156 Main St., St. Helena 94574. (707) 963-7736. Rentals available. Open Mon–Sat. 9:30–6.

Chiles Valley Loop 3a

EARNING YOUR WINE

Distance: 37 miles
Terrain: Very hilly. The toughest ride in this book, designed for those who regularly accept cycling challenges. Gearing in the 30s. Remember your water bottle, preferably filled with ERG.

Start at Sage Canyon Road (Highway 128), which goes east from the Silverado Trail about 5 miles north of Yountville and follows the edge of Lake Hennessey. Push up 8 miles (now don't say we didn't warn you, it's tough!); then the road starts downhill, following Sage Creek.

NICHELINI This old winery, snuggled against the road, pours generous samples of its country wines, but don't relax too much. Continue on a bit to Lower Chiles Valley Road and turn left there.

RUSTRIDGE A mile or so up this road on the right is a brand new winery run by the Meyer family. A thoroughbred ranch was converted to vineyards in 1974, and the new wines, first released in 1985, reflect the horsey heritage. They welcome cyclists and have picnic facilities.

In about 2 miles, this road reaches Chiles & Pope Valley Road. Turn right and ride another 8 miles to Howell Mountain Road, turn left and climb to Angwin. This is the steepest part, but the Angwin Market can supply a healthy picnic lunch.

The road starts down into Napa Valley after Angwin. Take Deer Park Road, left, at the intersection.

BURGESS CELLARS Descending, you'll see a small winery on the right, open daily for sales but no tasting. You'll probably want water, at this point, which Tom Burgess has—coming out of a garden hose! But there's nothing second class about the wines.

DEER PARK Continuing downhill, look for a vineyard and two stone pillars on your left and go up that driveway. This is another small operation also welcoming cyclists, and winemaker Dave Clark appreciates advance warning for serious attention to visitors. They also have overnight accommodations.

The stop sign at the bottom of the hill is the Silverado Trail. Turn left to return to where you started. Turn right to continue with Ride 3.

WINERIES TO VISIT

Burgess Cellars, 1108 Deer Park Rd., St. Helena 94574. (707) 963-4766. Open daily for sales, tours by appointment.

Deer Park Winery, 1000 Deer Park Rd., Deer Park 94576. (707) 963-5411. Be sure the "open" sign is out.

Nichelini Vineyard, 2950 Sage Canyon Rd., St. Helena 94574. (707) 963-3357. Open weekends or by appointment.

Rustridge Vineyards, 2910 Lower Chiles Valley Rd., St. Helena 94574. (707) 965-2871. Retail sales daily.

SELECTED STOPS

The College Market, Angwin. (707) 965-6321. Closed Saturday.

BICYCLE ASSISTANCE: You are on your own.

You can even drive these rides.

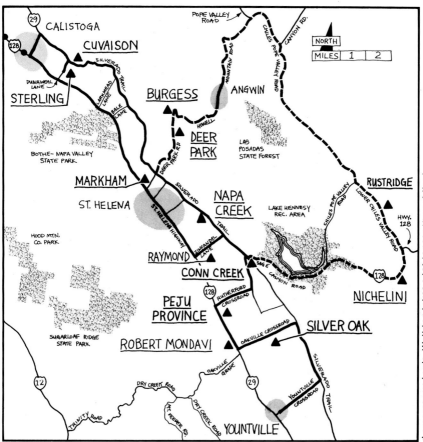

Be sure to carry a spare tube or tire and emergency tools. Walking takes a lot longer than riding!

4 Alexander Valley Loop

FIVE WINES & NO HILLS

Distance: 24 miles
Terrain: Nearly flat, with bridges and freeway overpasses for hills. Gearing in the 50s. Wind from the northwest in the afternoon.

Starting at Dry Creek Road and Highway 101, park at the Deli and load up on picnic supplies. Head east on Dry Creek Road, which ends at the light, Healdsburg Avenue. Turn left, away from Healdsburg, and your first winery stop is a mile up on the left.

SIMI Over 100 years old, this elegant stone facility, now owned by Moet Hennessy, offers tours and tastings daily. Cool redwood trees shade the picnic ground. You may want to save this for your return trip. Winemaker Zelma Long has created some excellent wines.

Turn right a little farther up the road onto Alexander Valley Road, and continue across the Russian River where this road merges with Highway 128. Follow this road as it turns right and starts south towards Napa. Skip the first winery you see; they prefer not having cyclists.

ALEXANDER VALLEY Just 2 miles farther south, on the left, is an original Victorian home where winemaker and winery owner Hank Wetzel, Jr., has been making wine for two decades. The house dates back to General Vallejo.

FIELD STONE In contrast, this modern facility, built into the hillside 2 miles farther south, is another happy country setting, with picnic tables, if you are ready for lunch.

There is plenty more cycling to do, though. Turn back up Highway 128, north through Jim Town, then right, in front of the Alexander Valley store. Continue on this peaceful country road (still Highway 128) another 6 miles to Geyserville. For an Italian family-style lunch, stop at Catelli's. Then head south on the main street, Old Redwood Highway, and follow it as it winds to either side of the freeway (101).

TRENTADUE About 3 miles south is the old "32" winery, started by Leo Trentadue in 1972. They offer good quality and good value, as well as a cool spot to take a break.

Cross under 101 again, on Independence Lane.

SOUVERAIN This impressive facility, one of the biggest operations in the valley, also has an excellent restaurant and a veranda overlooking the valley.

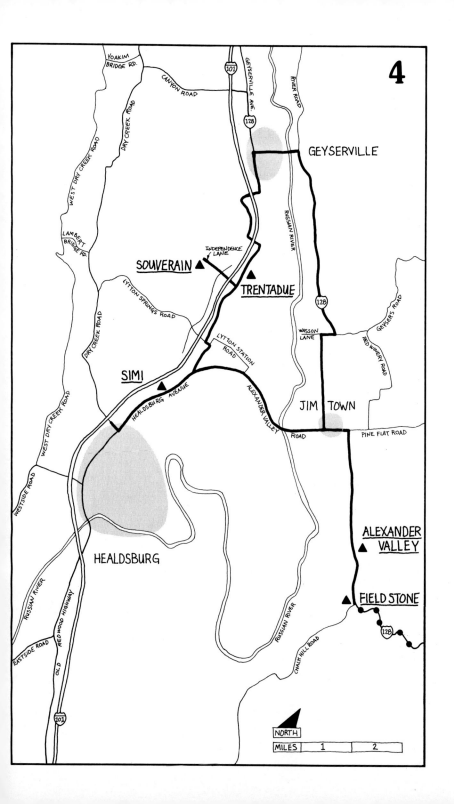

4

YOAKIM BRIDGE RD.

CANYON ROAD

101

GEYSERVILLE AVE.

128

RIVER ROAD

WEST DRY CREEK ROAD

DRY CREEK ROAD

GEYSERVILLE

RUSSIAN RIVER

LAMBERT BRIDGE RD.

INDEPENDENCE LANE

SOUVERAIN ▲

▲ **TRENTADUE**

128

LYTTON SPRINGS ROAD

DRY CREEK ROAD

WASSON LANE

GEYSERS ROAD

RED WINERY ROAD

LYTTON STATION ROAD

SIMI ▲

HEALDSBURG AVENUE

ALEXANDER VALLEY ROAD

JIM TOWN

PINE FLAT ROAD

WEST DRY CREEK ROAD

WESTSIDE ROAD

HEALDSBURG

ALEXANDER VALLEY ▲

▲ **FIELD STONE**

128

RUSSIAN RIVER

RUSSIAN RIVER

OLD REDWOOD HIGHWAY

EASTSIDE ROAD

CHALK HILL ROAD

101

NORTH

MILES 1 2

Go back to the Old Redwood Highway and continue south back to Healdsburg, stopping off at Simi for a final tasting, if you skipped it on your way out.

WINERIES TO VISIT

Alexander Valley Vineyards, 8644 Hwy. 128, Healdsburg 95448. (707) 433-7209. Open daily.

Field Stone Winery, 10075 Hwy. 128, Healdsburg 95448. (707) 433-7266. Picnic area. Call for summer concert schedule. Open daily.

Simi Winery, 16275 Healdsburg Ave., Healdsburg 95448. (707) 433-6981. Open daily.

Chateau Souverain, Independence Lane at Hwy. 101, Geyserville 95441. (707) 433-8281. Call restaurant for reservations: (707) 433-3141. Open daily.

Trentadue Winery, 19170 Redwood Hwy., Geyserville 95441. (707) 433-3104. Open daily.

SELECTED STOPS

Catelli's, Main St., Geyserville 95441. (707) 857-9904.

Camping: see Ride 5.

Bed & Breakfast: Isis Oasis, 20889 Geyserville Rd., Geyserville 95441. Weekend dinner theater. (707) 857-3524.

Camellia Inn, 211 North St., Healdsburg 95448. (707) 433-8182.

Frampton House, 489 Powell Ave., Healdsburg 95448. (707) 433-5084. Has bicycles.

Belle de Jour, 16276 Healdsburg Ave., Healdsburg 95448. (707) 433-7892.

Northern Wine Country Inns. (707) 433-INNS.

Russian River Wine Road, PO Box 127, Geyserville 95441. (707) 433-6935.

BICYCLE ASSISTANCE: Spoke Folk Cyclery, 249 Center St., Healdsburg 95448. (707) 433-7171. Open daily. Rental bikes available.

OVER HEALDS, OVER DALE

Distance: 20 miles
Terrain: Rolling hills. Gearing in the 40s. Not too difficult, but plan for prevailing afternoon winds from the northwest.

Starting in Healdsburg, again, at the Deli just off Highway 101 at Dry Creek Road, head west on Dry Creek Road towards Lake Sonoma. At the Dry Creek Store, stop for picnic supplies, then turn left onto Lambert Bridge Road and pass the first winery you see, as they prefer not having cyclists.

ROBERT STEMMLER In the small, friendly winery, making excellent estate wines from the grapes you see around you, Stemmler reflects his German heritage in the dry white wines and the medieval tapestry label. Call ahead if you want to picnic here, otherwise they are open for tasting daily, on the right.

Follow Lambert Bridge as it doglegs across Dry Creek, and turn right up West Dry Creek Road. This quiet country lane ambles north through vineyards and wineries open by appointment only.

PRESTON Near the very top, about 4 miles up, is another small, family operation started in 1977 by a family who had been growing grapes in the valley for generations. They request an appointment, but the office keeps regular weekday hours.

Backtrack ¼ mile to Yoakim Bridge Road and turn left, cross the valley, and turn left again onto Dry Creek Road.

FERRARI CARANO About 2 miles up, on the left, is the spanking new winery run by Steve Meisner—opened the summer of 1987.

Across the road from the winery, take Dutcher Creek Road north to Cloverdale, about 5 miles.

BANDIERA Just on the south edge of Cloverdale, where they still hold a Citrus Fair every February though the citrus trees died out years ago, you'll see the tasting room of this winery clearly marked, on the left. The winemaker, John Merritt, is an old hand at making good Sonoma County wines. The labels feature watercolors of California wildflowers, and packets of the whole collection are free of charge.

There are some interesting things in Cloverdale, but for more wine, retrace your steps back down Highway 101, staying on the east side (left) of 101 as it turns into freeway and bicycles are forbidden. This is the Old Redwood Highway, the road to Asti, a tiny town with two wineries.

PAT PAULSEN This comedian and perpetual presidential candidate has been seriously growing grapes in the area for 15 years. His winery's tasting room is now downtown Asti's number one attraction. Italian Swiss Colony is across the road, and there's a grocery/deli, too.

Continue south on Old Redwood Highway, towards Geyserville, but turn right at Canyon Road, crossing under Highway 101.

GEYSER PEAK You'll have to turn right into their driveway, just west of Highway 101. It's a much bigger operation now than it used to be, but the tasting room and picnic facilities overlook Alexander Valley and the wines are good.

Continue west on Canyon Road about a mile.

PEDRONCELLI One of the oldest and best winemaking families in the county, John and James, sons of the founder, and their children and grandchildren still make rich, dark reds and crisp, dry whites.

Follow the creekbed west until Canyon Road ends at Dry Creek Road and retrace your steps. You can follow West Dry Creek Road all the way back to Healdsburg, entering town on the south side, via Mill Street, if you don't mind doubling back through town to your car.

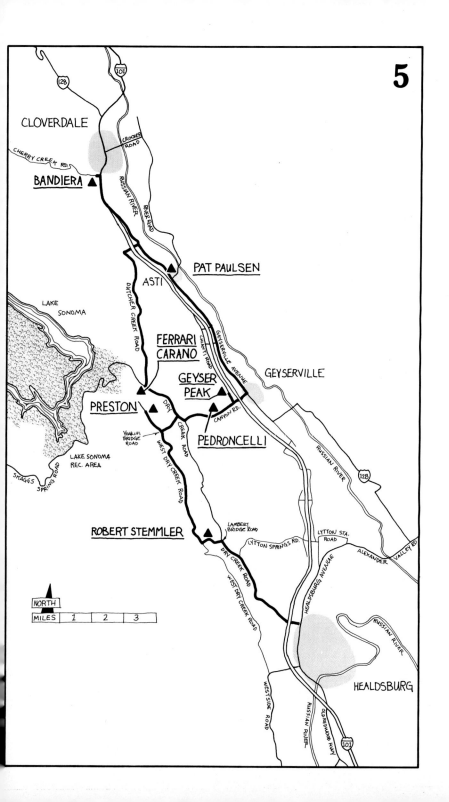

5

CLOVERDALE

CHERRY CREEK RD.

CROCKER ROAD

BANDIERA ▲

RUSSIAN RIVER

RIVER ROAD

PAT PAULSEN ▲

ASTI

DUTCHER CREEK ROAD

LAKE SONOMA

FERRARI CARANO

CHIANTI ROAD

GEYSERVILLE AVENUE

GEYSER PEAK ▲

GEYSERVILLE

PRESTON ▲

DRY CREEK ROAD

CANYON RD.

PEDRONCELLI

RUSSIAN RIVER

YOAKIM BRIDGE ROAD

WEST DRY CREEK ROAD

LAKE SONOMA REC. AREA

SKAGGS SPRING ROAD

128

ROBERT STEMMLER ▲

LAMBERT BRIDGE ROAD

LYTTON STA. ROAD

LYTTON SPRINGS RD.

ALEXANDER VALLEY RD.

DRY CREEK ROAD

WEST DRY CREEK ROAD

HEALDSBURG AVENUE

RUSSIAN RIVER

NORTH

MILES   1   2   3

WESTSIDE ROAD

RUSSIAN RIVER

OLD REDWOOD HWY

101

HEALDSBURG

WINERIES TO VISIT

Bandiera Winery (155 Cherry Creek Rd.). Tasting room: 555 S. Cloverdale Blvd., Cloverdale 95425. (707) 894-4295. Open daily.

Ferrari-Carano, 8761 Dry Creek Rd., Healdsburg 95448. (707) 433-6700. Tasting room opens August 1987.

Geyser Peak Winery, Canyon Rd. at Hwy. 101, Geyserville 95441. (707) 433-6585. Open daily.

Pat Paulsen Vineyards (25510 River Rd., Cloverdale 95425). Tasting room in Asti open daily. (707) 894-2969.

Pedroncelli Winery, 1220 Canyon Rd., Geyserville 95441. (707) 857-3531. Open daily.

Preston Vineyards, 9282 West Dry Creek Rd., Healdsburg 95448. (707) 433-3372. By appointment.

Robert Stemmler Wines, 3805 Lambert Bridge Rd., Healdsburg 95448. (707) 433-6334. Open daily. Picnics by reservation.

SELECTED STOPS

Camping: Cloverdale KOA, on Hwy. 101 6 miles south of town. (707) 894-3337.

Bed & Breakfast: The Campbell Ranch, 1475 Canyon Rd., Geyserville 95441. (707) 857-3476.

The Hope-Merrill House, 21253 Geyserville Ave., Geyserville 95441. (707) 857-3356.

Vintage Towers Inn, 302 N. Main St., Cloverdale 95425. (707) 894-4535.

Central B&B exchange: (707) 433-INNS.
(Also see B&B's listing in Ride 4.)

BICYCLE ASSISTANCE: Cloverdale Cyclery, 127 E. First St., Cloverdale 95425. (707) 894-2841. (See Ride 4, also.)

Healdsburg to Guerneville 6

EAST SIDE, WEST SIDE ROADS

Distance: 21 miles
Terrain: Rolling road going south, flat coming back. Gearing in the 40s.

Starting in Healdsburg again, visit one of the wineries tucked away off Mill Street, just south of the square.

CLOS DU BOIS Mill Street, east, ends at East Street; turn right, then left on Hayden, then right again on Fitch. Good wines, made from Alexander Valley grapes, and a friendly tasting room staff will make a good start for your tour.

Retrace your route back to Mill Street and follow that west, under Highway 101. It makes a left turn about a mile out of town and becomes Westside Road. Follow that south for the next 10 miles.

MILL CREEK Just after you turn onto Westside Road, on the right, is the Kreck family winery. It was here that the term "Blush" was first coined by the winemaker.

BELVEDERE About 2 miles farther is a new winery, just opened for tasting. They even have a bike rack. The old Victorian house is an original.

HOP KILN WINERY A mile farther is another winery featuring bicycle parking. The three-towered hop kiln barn, an echo of the former crop of the North Coast used in traditional beer-making, is the symbol and the name for this winery. Dr. Martin Griffin is the owner. You can picnic in the shade of the barn by a pond.

J. ROCHIOLI Next door, an old-time vineyard family has turned to wine-making as well. If Hop Kiln is crowded, try this smaller, newer operation for tasting and picnicking.

DAVIS BYNUM Another mile along Westside Road, on the right, the father and son team of Davis and Hampton make everything from "Barefoot Bynum" jug wines to vintaged Pinot Noir on which they sell futures. Follow the driveway back up the canyon to the barn for tastings.

6

One short climb follows, on Westside Road, before the left turn onto Wohler Road. This crosses the Russian River. Turn left again, a mile later, onto Eastside Road, and the return loop back to Healdsburg.

MARK WEST The climb in the first mile crests at Trenton-Healdsburg Road. If you take that right, in ½ mile, this winery is available for picnics and tasting. Otherwise, keep straight on Eastside Road.

PIPER-SONOMA In 3 more miles, Eastside Road ends at Old Redwood Highway. Turn left here. The French Champagne firm, Piper-Heidsieck, offers their California edition. It's about time for some bubbly!

SONOMA VINEYARDS Just beyond Piper is an all-American firm, run by Rodney Strong, also open to the public.

FOPPIANO This is a fine old Sonoma County wine family, still making great wines, though far more "high-tech" than in granddad's day. The setting is still the family home.

Follow Old Redwood Highway back into Healdsburg and turn up Mill Street to get back to where you started.

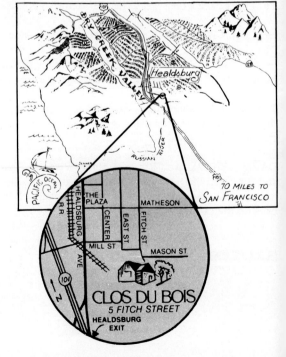

"My only regret in life is that I did not drink more champagne," said John Maynard Keynes.

36

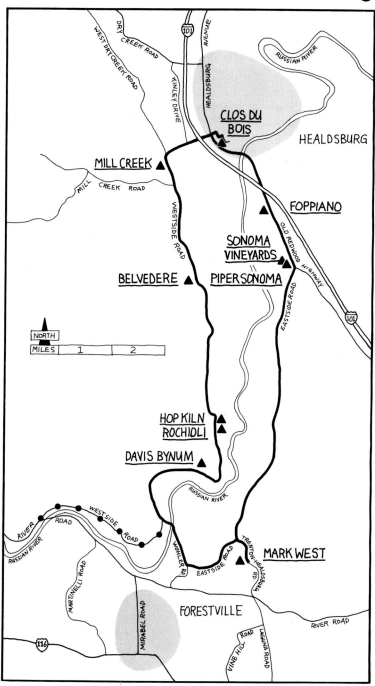

WINERIES TO VISIT

Belevedere Winery, 4035 Westside Rd., Healdsburg 95448. (707) 433-8236. Open daily. Bike rack.

Davis Bynum Winery, 8075 Westside Rd., Healdsburg 95448. (707) 433-5852. Open daily.

Clos du Bois, 5 Fitch St., Healdsburg 95448. (707) 433-5576. Open daily.

Foppiano Vineyards, 12707 Old Redwood Hwy., Healdsburg 95448. (707) 433-7272.

Hop Kiln Winery, 6050 Westside Rd., Healdsburg 95448. (707) 433-6491. Open daily.

Mark West Vineyards, 7000 Trenton-Healdsburg Rd., Forestville 95436. (707) 544-4813. Open daily. Picnic facilities.

Mill Creek Vineyards, 1401 Westside Rd., Healdsburg 95448. (707) 433-5098. Closed Mon-Tues in Dec-Mar.

Piper-Sonoma Cellars, 11447 Old Redwood Hwy., Healdsburg 95448. (707) 433-8843.

J. Rochioli Vineyard, 6192 Westside Rd., Healdsburg 95448. (707) 433-2305.

Sonoma Vineyards, 11455 Old Redwood Hwy., Healdsburg 95448. (707) 433-6511. Open daily.

SELECTED STOPS

Bed & Breakfast: Madrona House, 1001 Westside Rd., Healdsburg 95448. (707) 433-4231.

The Raford House, 10630 Wohler Rd. Healdsburg 95448. (707) 887-9573.

Central B&B Exchange: (707) 433-INNS.

BICYCLE ASSISTANCE: See Ride 4.

The Russian River 7

GUERNEVILLE TO FORESTVILLE . . . AND BACK!

Distance: 27 miles
Terrain: Hilly on Hwy. 116. Gearing in the 40s.

KORBEL Start here; they have ample parking and great sparkling wines to celebrate your return later in the day. The Heck family still runs this winery. Third-generation Gary Heck is in charge. Take the tour for a fascinating look at champagne and brandy processing.

Continue on River Road to Guerneville, an old resort town that is enjoying a revival. Cross the Russian River here, onto Highway 116 south, the Gravenstein Highway. It winds south through redwood-covered hills towards the apple country. It's about 7 miles to Forestville. Just as you get there, turn left onto Martinelli Road.

DOMAINE LAURIER Just up on the left, this small winery has some lovely wines. They are open Saturdays, or by appointment.

Return to Highway 116 and continue through Forestville.

TOPOLOS AT RUSSIAN RIVER The mock hop kiln architecture of this progressive winery is on the right, just south of town. The winemaker, Michael Topolos, will often pour the wine downstairs in the tasting room. Upstairs is a good restaurant and a cool patio with tables outside.

Just another mile south, again on the right, is Ross Station Road. Make an appointment in advance to visit the winery at the far end.

IRON HORSE The old Victorian farmhouse, beautifully restored by the Sterlings, is now surrounded by vineyards. This was once a horse farm and home of Roy Roger's Trigger.

Continuing on 116 to the Guerneville Road, on the left, turn here. The signs will point to Santa Rosa.

DEHLINGER Tom and his family offer their wines daily for tasting, just up the road at the corner of Vine Hill.

DE LOACH Two more miles along Guerneville Road, turn left at Olivet and in another mile stop at another small family operation, on the left.

Continue on Oliver north, another mile, to River Road. Turn left and go back along the river to Guerneville.

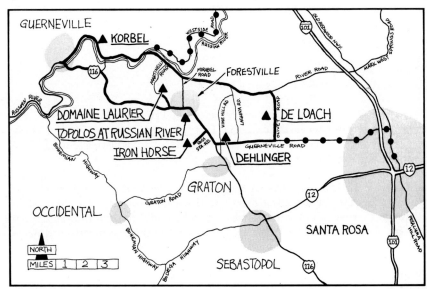

WINERIES TO VISIT

Dehlinger Winery, 6300 Guerneville Rd., Sebastopol 95472. (707) 823-2378. Open 1–4:30, weekdays; 10–5, Sat-Sun.

De Loach Vineyards, 1791 Olivet Rd., Santa Rosa 95401. (707) 526-9111. Open daily.

Domaine Laurier, 8075 Martinelli Rd., Forestville 95436. (707) 887-2176. Open Sat. 11–4, or by appointment.

Iron Horse Vineyards, 9786 Ross Station Rd., Sebastopol 95472. (707) 887-2913. By appointment only.

Korbel Brothers Champagne Cellars, 13250 Old River Rd., Guerneville 95446. (707) 887-2294. Open daily.

Topolos at Russian River Vineyards, 5700 Gravenstein Hwy. North, Forestville 94536. (707) 887-1563. Restaurant open daily in summer, weekends in winter. (707) 887-1562.

SELECTED STOPS

Camping: River Bend Trailer Park, 11820 River Rd. (1 mile E. of Korbel), Guerneville 95446. (707) 887-7662.

Bed & Breakfast: Creekside Inn, 16180 Neeley Rd., Guerneville 95446. (707) 869-3623.

The Estate, 13555 Hwy. 116, Guerneville 95446. (707) 869-9093.

Paradise Cove, 14711 Armstrong Woods Rd., Guerneville 95446. (707) 869-2706.

Ridenhour Ranch House Inn, 12850 River Rd., Guerneville 95446. (707) 887-1033.

BICYCLE ASSISTANCE: Bike Peddlar, 530 McConnell Ave., Santa Rosa 95404. (707) 544-0868.

Mendocino County 8

A BIG HOP TO UKIAH AND BACK

Distance: Up to 52 miles, depending on how far you get from Hopland.
Terrain: Flat to rolling hills. Gearing in the 40–50s. East Side Road has little shoulder but hardly any traffic. Highway 101 allows bikes but is uncomfortable cycling. Winds from the north in the afternoon.

Start in the thriving wine town of Hopland (once a great source of hops for beer-making) at the intersection of Highways 101 and 175, going east.

FETZER The parking lot at Fetzer's Wine Tasting facility (once the town's schoolhouse) is a good place to leave your car and stock up on picnic supplies. The 11 descendants of the founder of this winery all work, in one way or another, for this most successful Mendocino County wine operation. They have turned Hopland into wineland. The school gymnasium is now a restaurant, and the wines are among the best of the north country style.

McDOWELL VALLEY VINEYARDS Take Highway 175 to East Hopland, passing East Side Road, Route 201, on the left. About 4 miles out 175, on the left, is the world's first solar-integrated winery. The facility is striking, and they welcome picnickers. You might be lucky and hit one of their food-with-wine days. They also have a tasting room in Hopland.

To continue on to Ukiah and the wineries there, return towards Hopland, taking East Side Road north, a right turn just inside East Hopland. The scenery is superb: vineyards, grazing sheep and horses, and a quiet country road all the way to Talmage, about 10 miles. At the Talmage store, on your right, turn left onto Talmage Road, which crosses the freeway into Ukiah, about 2 miles away.

HIDDEN CELLARS WINERY Halfway to Ukiah, on the left, take Cunningham Road, which makes a right angle a quarter mile down at this new winery, started by Dennis Patton in 1981. They make 100-percent varietal wines.

You can continue down this road back to East Side Road and Hopland.

Alternate Long Route

Brave State Street, Ukiah, always full of pickup trucks, or follow the parallel streets through town, north.

CRESTA BLANCA Though they are based in the San Jose area, their wine-making facility here, just north of Ukiah on North State Street and just beyond the 101 underpass, sports a nice little tasting room. One of the oldest California labels (see Livermore Ride 9), Cresta Blanca wines include some good varietals. Give them a try before continuing on to an old Mendocino County family winery.

PARDUCCI Continuing another half mile up North State Street, look for Parducci Road on your left, and follow it back over the freeway. The winery has 40 different wines, and family members often pour in the cool tasting room.

You can continue on North State Street up to Calpella. It's a pretty country road, once it finally gets beyond the trailer parks and fast-food outlets of Ukiah. Weibel, another San Francisco Bay area winery, has a fancy tasting room at the very end, about 4 miles up, where the road feeds into Highway 101. Ask about their grape stomp in September. This makes a long day's ride!

JEPSON Returning to Hopland, via East Side Road and Highway 175, brave Highway 101 north of town for about 3 miles to reach this brand-new Mendocino County winery and taste its first release in 1987.

MILANO Or if you prefer, another small winery, with a very original winery building and tasting room, is less than a mile south of Hopland on the right. The driveway is steep and gravelly, but the wines are easy.

Whichever, don't miss, after a day's wine tasting, a cold Hopland Brewery beer.

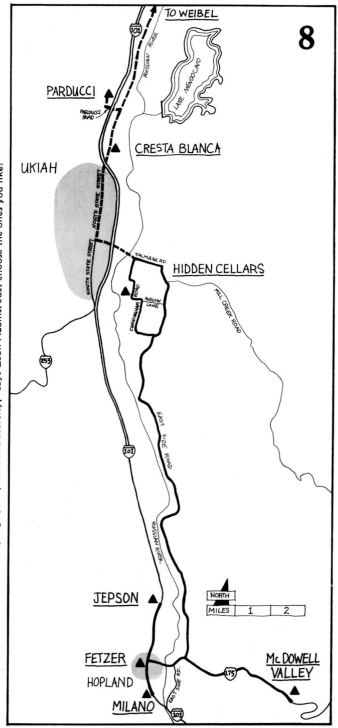

"Wine taste is preconditioned by high price, fame and scarcity," says Leon Adams. Just choose the ones you like!

WINERIES TO VISIT

Cresta Blanca Vineyards, 2399 North State Street, Ukiah 95482. (707) 462-2987. Open daily.

Fetzer Vineyards Wine Tasting, 13500 South Hwy. 101, Hopland 95449. (707) 744-1737. Open daily.

Hidden Cellars Winery, 1500 Cunningham Rd., Ukiah 95482. (PO Box 448, Talmage 95481) (707) 462-0301. Open daily, Jun–Oct; weekdays in winter.

Jepson Vineyards, 10400 So. Hwy. 101, Ukiah 95482. (707) 468-8936.

McDowell Valley Vineyards, 3811 Hwy. 175, Hopland 95449. (707) 744-1053. Open daily.

Milano Winery, 14594 So. Hwy. 101, Hopland 95449. (707) 744-1396.

Parducci Wine Cellars, 501 Parducci Rd., Ukiah 95482. (707) 462-9463.

Weibel, Redwood Valley at Hwy. 101. (707) 485-0321. (1250 Stanford Ave., Mission San Jose 94539. [415] 656-2340.)

SELECTED STOPS

Bluebird Cafe, Hwy. 101, Hopland 95449.

Ed Knott's General Store, Hopland 95449.

Palace Hotel, 272 North State St., Ukiah 95482. (707) 468-9291.

Lake Mendocino Campgrounds, North State St., Ukiah 95482. (707) 462-7581.

Mendocino Brewing Co., Hwy. 101, Hopland 95449. (707) 744-1015. Open daily from 11, with live music on weekends.

Thatcher Lodge, Hwy. 101, Hopland 95449. (707) 744-1061.

BICYCLE ASSISTANCE: Draper's Raleigh Cycles, 846 South State St., Ukiah 95482. (707) 462-3230.

Ukiah Schwinn, Gobbi St., Ukiah 95482. (707) 462-2686. Closed Sundays.

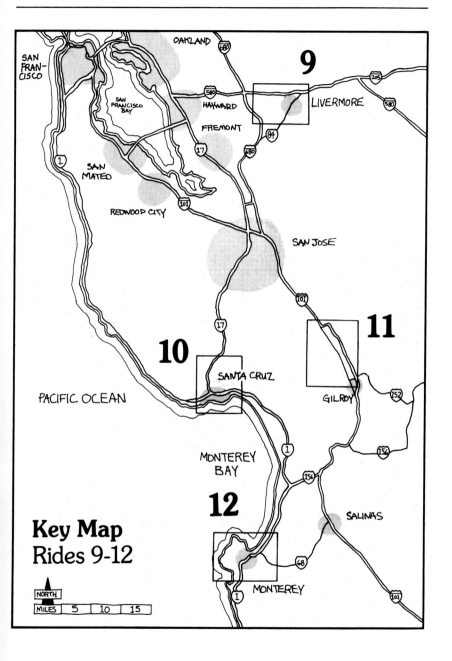

Key Map
Rides 9-12

NORTH
MILES 5 10 15

9 Livermore Valley

THE COUNTRYSIDE BY INTERSTATE 580

Distance: **20 miles**
Terrain: Nearly flat with a few rolls and an afternoon wind out of the west. Start at Wente and enjoy a wind to your back on the way home.

Getting there: Interstate 580. Take Livermore or Pleasanton exits.

WENTE BROS.   Start at the original family winery on Tesla Road, taking South Vasco Road from 580 and turning right onto Tesla. Park at the winery, ½ mile up on the left. Now run by the fourth generation, Eric, Phil and Carolyn Wente, this 104-year-old operation is still innovating—wait until you taste their sparkling wine!

CONCANNON   Back on Tesla Road, just a bit farther down, is another old family winery, with an Irish heritage unusual in the wine business. James Concannon beat the Wentes to the neighborhood by one year, but the family has now sold the business to a British firm. With the infusion of money from the new investors, look for some interesting changes.

Proceeding again along Tesla, which doglegs to the right and becomes Livermore Avenue, go to the end of the neatly managed Concannon vineyards and turn right.

RETZLAFF   The driveway leading to this charming little winery follows the edge of Concannon vineyards a short way, then down a grassy lane to the left. The tasting room and grassy picnic lawn are actually the backside of the winery. Husband and wife team, Robert and Gloria Retzlaff Taylor, usually greet visitors. Gloria will also cater picnic lunches for groups of 10 or more, if you call her in advance. Their Grey Reisling, from a white grape of the Bordeaux region of France, and their Chardonnay are made in the French style.

Backtrack 100 yards on Livermore and take Wente Street to the right. Follow Wente through peaceful back country until it right-angles at Marina, and follow Marina to Arroyo Road. Turn left on Arroyo and head for the hills, passing the future site of the Livermore Valley Wine Museum.

The road will descend into the valley where Charles Wetmore first planted his California "Sauternes" in 1882. His Cresta Blanca white wine won a gold medal at the Paris Exposition of 1889, officially putting the state on the world wine map.

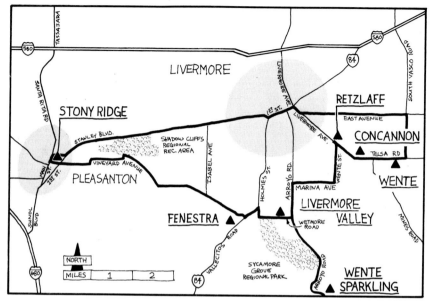

WENTE SPARKLING WINE CELLARS Two miles down this pretty country road is the handsome new winery, with a cool and spacious tasting room, a sandstone aging cellar, a French country restaurant, and pleasing sparkling wine fit for a celebration—or a day cycling in the vineyards.

Take a rest here, as the only way back is up the hill you just cruised down. Once at the top of Arroyo, where the old gateway to "Olivina" still stands, turn left onto Wetmore Road. Julius Smith spent the fortune he made with 20-Mule Team Borax building Olivina, but, like most fortunes, little remains.

LIVERMORE VALLEY Zipping down Wetmore, turn right into the first driveway, where Chris Lagiss, an old-hand at winemaking, now makes his own with the help of his family.

Wetmore ends, after a dogleg to the right, at East Vallecitos Road. The cars are fast here. There is a shoulder, except across a narrow bridge. Turn left and go about 1 mile up and look for an old swaybacked barn on the right.

FENESTRA Although Lanny and Fran Replogle have been here for seven years, they only recently opened the winery for regular weekend tastings. The driveway and parking lot are dirt, so walk your bike down to the winery barn.

Return the way you came to Wente, or continue with the longer, alternate route.

Alternate Route

For a longer ride, and one more tasting room, take Vineyard Avenue, the first left on East Vallecitos as you return from Fenestra, and ride 12 miles to Pleasanton. You have to make a left-hand jog, and the rapidly developing town cannot be recommended highly, but Vineyard will get you to Main Street and the tasting room of Stony Ridge, just behind the Cheese Store, across the street from the Pleasanton Hotel. Take Stanley Boulevard back to Livermore, through the developments, or backtrack on the quieter Vineyard Avenue. The wind will be at your back.

WINERIES TO VISIT

Concannon Vineyard, 4590 Tesla Rd., Livermore 94550. (415) 447-3700. Open daily except Sunday morning.

Fenestra Winery, 83 East Vallecitos Rd., Livermore 94550. (415) 447-5246. Open Thurs–Sun, 12–5.

Livermore Valley Cellars, 1508 Wetmore Rd., Livermore 94550. (415) 447-1751. Open daily, 10–5.

Retzlaff Vineyards, 1356 South Livermore Ave., Livermore 94550. (415) 447-8941. Open Wed–Sun, 11–5.

Wente Bros., 5565 Tesla Rd., Livermore 94550. (415) 447-3606. Open daily except Sunday morning.

Wente Bros. Sparkling Wine Cellars, 5050 Arroyo Rd., Livermore 94550. (415) 447-3023. Open daily, 11–5:30. Restaurant open Wed–Sun for lunch and dinner. Reservations advised: (415) 447-3696.

SELECTED STOPS

Camping: Lake Del Valle State Recreation Area, 10 miles south of Livermore on Via Tesla, Mines and Del Valle roads. (415) 443-4110.

Pleasanton Hotel, 855 Main St., Pleasanton 94566. (415) 846-8106.

BICYCLE ASSISTANCE: Livermore Cyclery, 2288 First St., Livermore 94550. (415) 455-8090.

Sparkling Wine Cellars of Wente

10 Santa Cruz

DOWN BY THE SEA, WITH WINE

Distance: 16 miles
Terrain: Slight grade to Soquel, then a few steep climbs on the way back, with wonderful views to distract you.

Starting at San Lorenzo Park in Santa Cruz, take Dakota Avenue to Ocean, then left one block to Water Street. Turn left again onto Water, then take the first right, onto River Street.

FRICK WINERY The third left is Potrero, and Frick Winery, not a particularly fancy operation, but devotees will enjoy the wine talk as much as the wine tasting. Be sure to call first for an appointment.

Now return to Water Street and follow it to Soquel.

Water Street becomes Soquel Avenue and in 2 miles crosses Highway 1. Take the left fork onto Soquel Drive and follow it into town.

BARGETTO Turn left onto Main Street. About ½ mile up on the left is this family's fine collection of wines and related goodies. If you've had a prejudice against fruit wines, you'll lose it here. Try them, and the varietal wines, too!

BOUDON-SMITH Turn back down Main, cross Soquel Drive, and look for your next tasting opportunity on the right. These are varietals, mostly, from their own vineyards.

DEVLIN If you want still more wine discoveries, return to Soquel Drive, turn right, and at the intersection with Park Avenue, turn left. Follow this road up ½ mile, staying to the left (there will be grape clusters to mark the turns). The road ends at the steep driveway to this home and winery. Call first to arrange a visit, but they are usually there on weekends.

Otherwise, turn right on Park from Soquel Drive and continue around to the beach and back to where you started. Pass under Highway 1; be sure to look up at the view! When Park runs into Monterey Avenue, turn left and slide down to the Esplanade. This will carry you across the Soquel River and along Cliff Drive, which becomes East Cliff Drive.

When you reach Lake Avenue turn right, proceed to Murray Street where you turn left. Murray becomes East Cliff Drive and farther on, San Lorenzo Blvd. At the end of San Lorenzo turn right onto Riverside, which becomes Dakota, and, *voila*, you're back, or else you got lost somewhere back when one of the roads changed its name for the third time.

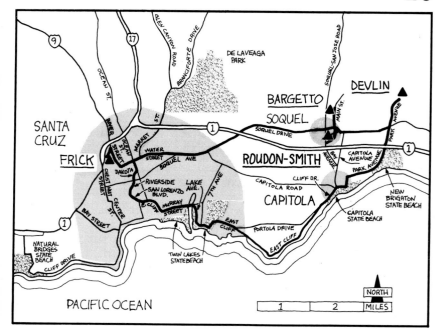

If you get lost, take heart and ask the way to the Santa Cruz Brewing Company in downtown Santa Cruz on Front Street. Console yourself in this local brew. The producers are a former winemaking father and son team, Bernie and Gerry Turgeon.

51

WINERIES TO VISIT

Bargetto Winery, 3535-A North Main St., Soquel 95073. (408) 475-2258. Open daily, 9–6.

Devlin Wine Cellars, Park Ave. (PO Box 728), Soquel 95073. (408) 476-7288. Open Sat–Sun, 12–5, or by appointment.

Frick Winery, 303 Potrero, #39, Santa Cruz 95060. (408) 426-8623. Open for tastings Sat, 12–5.

Roudon-Smith Winery (Tasting room: 2571 Main St., Soquel 95073). (408) 438-1244. Open Wed–Sun, 12–6.

SELECTED STOPS

Camping: Henry Cowell Redwoods State Park, 3 mi. north of Santa Cruz via Graham Hill Rd. (408) 335-4598.

New Brighton State Beach, Hwy. 1 in Capitola. (408) 475-4850.

Santa Cruz Bed & Breakfast hotline: (408) 425-8212.

Santa Cruz Brewing Co., 516 Front St., Santa Cruz 95060. (408) 429-8838. Open daily, 11:30 to midnight.

BICYCLE ASSISTANCE: Dutchman Bicycles, 3961 Portola Dr., Santa Cruz 95060. (408) 476-9555.

Bicycle Center, 1420 Mission St., Santa Cruz 95060. (408) 423-6324.

Appellations do not come from Appalachia.

MT. MADONNA TO MORGAN HILL

Distance: 29 miles
Terrain: Rolling hills, with afternoon winds out of the north. Gearing in the 30s.

Start on "Winery Row." Take the Hecker Pass (Highway 152) from 101 and go west about 4 miles.

HECKER PASS The last winery in the row, ½ mile beyond Watsonville Road on the right, is a good place to start. This is one of the original Fortino family wineries. The wines are still made in the Italian tradition, and include sherry and port. Park here and begin, heading back to Watsonville Road.

FORTINO Brother Ernest runs the winery next door, which was purchased from the Cassa family in 1970.

Just beyond Fortino, on the same side of Highway 152, is Watsonville Road (G8). Turn here and go 2 miles to the next winery stop.

KIRIGIN Featuring wines of the beautiful Uvas Valley, the Kirigin family bought this old Bonesio Winery in 1976. It's up on the hill, just at the corner of Day Road.

SYCAMORE CREEK Just another mile up Watsonville Road, at Uvas Road, turn to the left and descend on the driveway of the old Marchetti family winery, established in 1906 and now owned by Terry and Mary Parks. A lovely spot for a picnic.

Continue on Watsonville to the left turn at Sycamore. In 2 miles Sycamore ends at Oak Glen Avenue. Turn left and follow this road. It is all pretty back country but with a few real hills. In 4 miles go right on Willow Springs, which will descend into the town of Morgan Hill, making a T at Hale Avenue. Go south (right) on Hale until you reach Main Avenue and turn left. Continue on Main to Monterey (Business 101). Turn right and proceed, carefully, until you reach Dunne Avenue. Turn left onto Dunne and proceed until you reach Murphy Avenue. Turn right and proceed one block to San Pedro Avenue.

PEDRIZZETTI This is another family operation; the matriarch is Phyllis, whose father-in-law bought the operation in 1945. They have a wide selection of wines, including a sparkler.

Return to Highway 101 (business) and continue south to the town of San Martin, about 5 miles.

SAN MARTIN This is by far the biggest winery in the area. Winemaker Ron Niino makes his Monterey and Santa Clara grapes into wines in the European style. There's a full deli in the tasting room, with chilled wines and picnic basket lunches.

Follow San Martin Avenue west, crossing back over business 101, and turn left at Coolidge Avenue, where San Martin ends. Continue south as the road jogs right and left, changing names to Turlock, Murphy, Morey and Santa Teresa. At Highway 152 turn right.

A. CONROTTO Just ¼ mile up on the left is this old family establishment, which welcomes cyclists on weekends. There are several more wineries along Hecker Pass, but by now you'll be ready to cover the last 3 miles back to Hecker Pass Winery and your ride-end toast.

WINERIES TO VISIT
A. Conrotto, 1690 Hecker Pass (Hwy. 152), Gilroy 95020. (408) 842-3053. Weekends only.
Fortino Winery, 4525 Hecker Pass (Hwy. 152), Gilroy 95020. (408) 842-3305.
Hecker Pass Winery, 4605 Hecker Pass (Hwy. 152), Gilroy 95020. (408) 842-8755.
Kirigin Cellars, 11550 Watsonville Rd., Gilroy 95020. (408) 847-8827.
Pedrizzetti Winery, 1645 San Pedro Ave., Morgan Hill 95037. (408) 779-7389.
San Martin Winery, 12900 Monterey Rd., San Martin 95046. (408) 683-2672.
Sycamore Creek Vineyards, 12775 Uvas Rd., Morgan Hill 95037. (408) 779-4738.

SELECTED STOPS
Camping: Henry W. Coe State Park, Dunne Ave., 15 mi. east of Hwy. 101. (408) 779-2728.
Uvas Canyon Co. Park, Road G8, Gilroy 95020. (408) 779-9232.

BICYCLE ASSISTANCE: Morgan Hill Bike Shop, 16825 Monterey Hwy., Morgan Hill 95037. (408) 779-4015. Open daily.

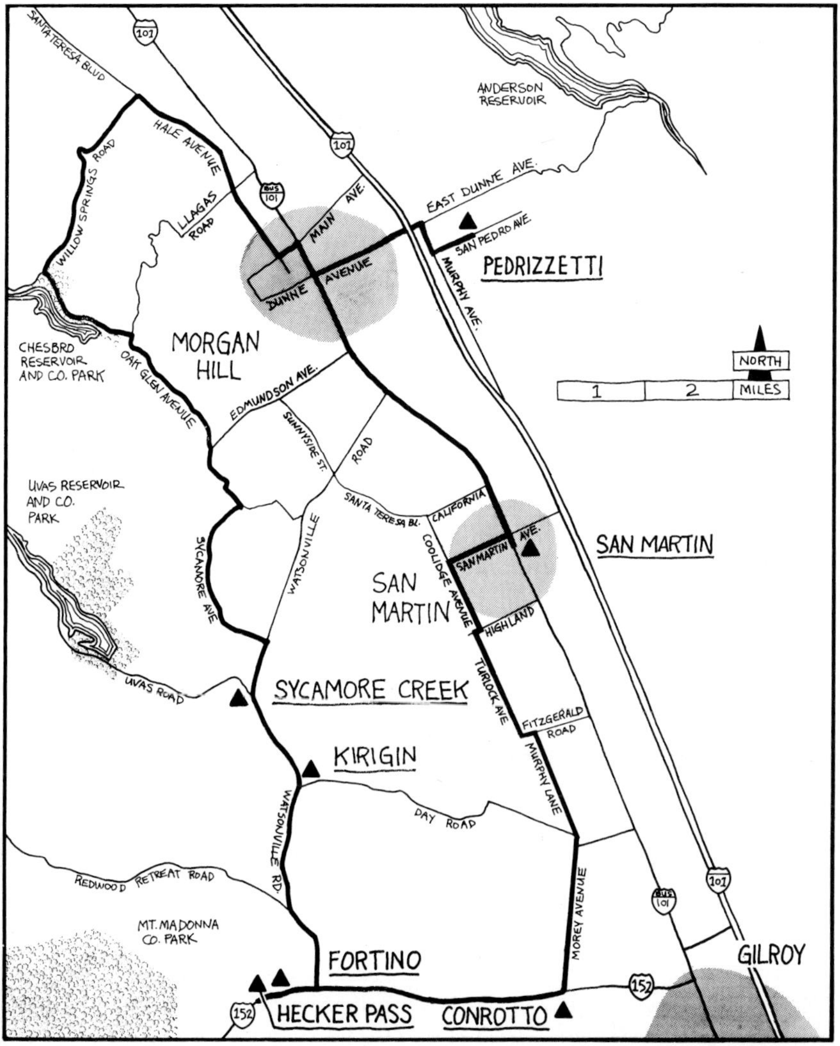
SANTA TERESA BLVD
101
HALE AVENUE
WILLOW SPRINGS ROAD
LLAGAS ROAD
BUS 101
MAIN AVE.
DUNNE AVENUE
ANDERSON RESERVOIR
EAST DUNNE AVE.
SAN PEDRO AVE.
PEDRIZZETTI
MURPHY AVE.
CHESBRO RESERVOIR AND CO. PARK
OAK GLEN AVENUE
MORGAN HILL
EDMUNDSON AVE.
SUNNYSIDE ST.
ROAD
NORTH
1
2
MILES
UVAS RESERVOIR AND CO. PARK
SANTA TERESA BL.
CALIFORNIA
SAN MARTIN AVE.
SAN MARTIN
SYCAMORE AVE
WATSONVILLE
COOLIDGE AVENUE
SAN MARTIN
HIGHLAND
UVAS ROAD
SYCAMORE CREEK
TURLOCK AVE
FITZGERALD ROAD
KIRIGIN
MURPHY LANE
WATSONVILLE RD.
DAY ROAD
REDWOOD RETREAT ROAD
MT. MADONNA CO. PARK
MOREY AVENUE
BUS 101
101
GILROY
FORTINO
152
152
HECKER PASS
CONROTTO

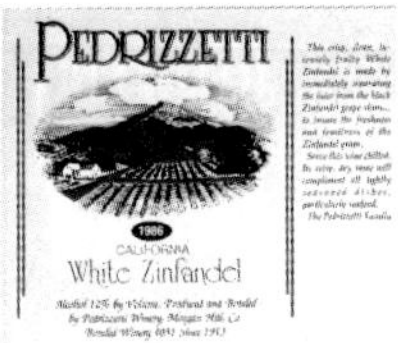
PEDRIZZETTI
1986
CALIFORNIA
White Zinfandel

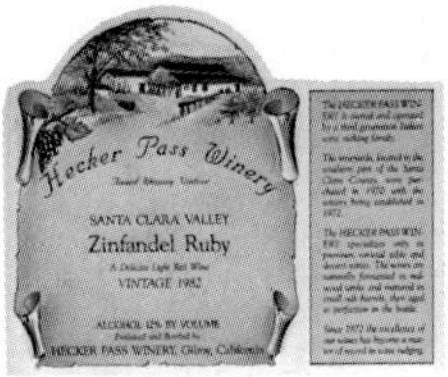
Hecker Pass Winery
SANTA CLARA VALLEY
Zinfandel Ruby
VINTAGE 1982
ALCOHOL 12% BY VOLUME
HECKER PASS WINERY, Gilroy, California

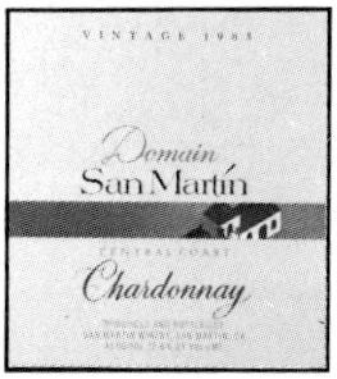
Domain
San Martín
Chardonnay

12 Monterey

SIPPING ALONG CANNERY ROW

Distance: 24 miles with a 4-mile weekday extension.

This is a tour of the Monterey Peninsula, with a beginning and end at the tasting rooms of three nearby wineries, all in Cannery Row. Park in one of the many lots around Cannery Row and take either Wave Street or Cannery Row towards Pacific Grove. The old Southern Pacific Railroad right-of-way just above Cannery Row has been converted into a hiking and biking path, running from Pt. Pinos to Seaside.

BARGETTO The winery's tasting room is in the Steinbeck Building in Cannery Row, right on the water. Across the street, at the corner of Cannery Row and Prescott, a commercial wine tasting center, The Wine Market, offers a good range of local and not-so-local wines.

MONTEREY PENINSULA Go up one street, to Wave, and look for a cute little Victorian cottage on the sea side. Try their robust Zinfandels and Barberas.

Continue towards Pacific Grove on the bike path, which follows Ocean View Boulevard with the advantage of the view without the traffic. At Asilomar Boulevard turn left, and continue to the left as it becomes Sunset Drive.

Weekday Alternate

If it's midweek, bicycles are allowed to turn right onto the 17-Mile Drive. Turn off at Carmel Gate and descent into Carmel for lunch.

Weekend riders must continue along Sunset Drive, which becomes Pacific Grove and then Carmel Hwy. After the long climb, when you have finally reached the intersection of Hwy. 1, take a breather. Now comes the tricky part. There is no alternative road to this section of the freeway, so you are allowed to ride on the shoulder of the highway. You'll see the sign designating it a Bikecentennial bike route.

The freeway becomes an ordinary busy road in about ½ mile. Be careful and turn right onto Carpenter Street, which takes you right down into Carmel. You'll be ready for a meal, no doubt, and you'll have plenty of places from which to choose.

Take the first right onto Munras Avenue and follow that around to Pacific. Turn right at Pacific and go back to Cannery Row via Foam.

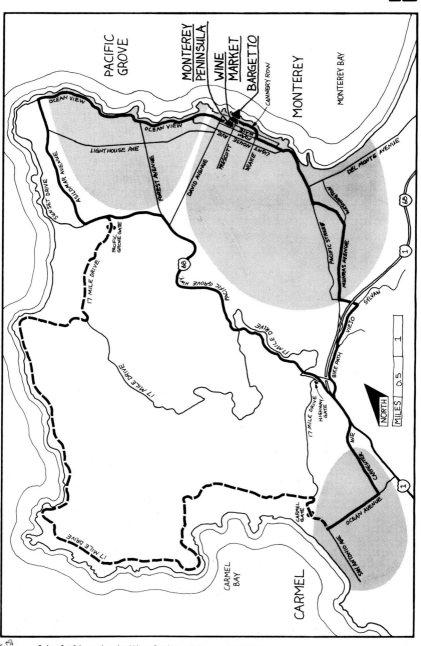

A loaf of bread, a bottle of wine and a . . . bicycle!

WINERIES TO VISIT

Bargetto Winery Tasting Room, 700 Cannery Row, Monterey 93940. (408) 373-4053.

Monterey Peninsula Winery Tasting Room, 786 Wave St., Monterey 93940. (408) 372-4949.

The Wine Market, Prescott at Cannery Row, Monterey 93940. (408) 375-6551.

SELECTED STOPS

Bed & Breakfast: The Jabberwock, 598 Laine St., Monterey 93940. (408) 372-4777.

The House of Seven Gables Inn, 555 Ocean View Blvd., Pacific Grove 93950. (408) 372-4341.

BICYCLE ASSISTANCE: Aquarian Bicycles, 444 Washington, Monterey 93940. (408) 375-2144. Closed Sunday and Monday mornings.

Joselyn's Bicycles, 638 Lighthouse Ave., Monterey 93940. (408) 649-8520. Closed Sun–Mon. Have rentals.

Seven Gables Inn

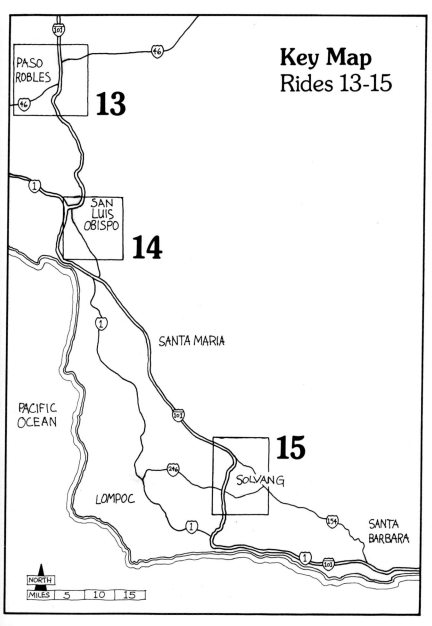

Key Map
Rides 13-15

13

14

15

PASO
ROBLES

SAN
LUIS
OBISPO

SANTA MARIA

PACIFIC
OCEAN

SOLVANG

LOMPOC

SANTA
BARBARA

NORTH

MILES | 5 | 10 | 15

13 Paso Robles

THE PASS OF THE OAKS

Distance: 34 miles
Terrain: Two fairly steep hills, one southwest and one northeast of town, and great downhill, open country stretches, including 1½ miles of dirt road. Gearing in the 40s.

The town of Paso Robles still manages a touch of the old west, in spite of the inevitable development of tract homes. The hills on either side of town grow great wine grapes, and it is here you will find the wineries. Start in Paso Robles, at the Chamber of Commerce on Spring Street, or next door at the great old Paso Robles Inn. A new batch of wineries, north of town, make an excellent morning tour.

Take 13th Street, just north of the CofC, and turn right, which leads across Highway 101 and the Salinas River. Just after the bridge, where Creston Road starts up the hill, turn left onto North River Road, and take the first right onto Union Road. This is a 1-mile climb up to the open country and the vineyards.

EBERLE Union Road touches Highway 46 East. Get on the shoulder of this fast throughway, and ½ mile east, on the left, is this new winery, run by Gary Eberle, the former winemaker at Estrella River. They make Cabernet, Chardonnay and a sweet Muscat Canelli. The grapes come from the vineyards of Howie Steinbeck, who is a partner. Even the watchdogs at the winery welcome cyclists.

ARCIERO Continuing out Highway 46, stay on the wide shoulder, and the fancy new complex of this Italian family is just 2 miles up on the right. You can't miss it, as they say. In fact, the first entrance, which looks like it might be the winery, is only the vineyard manager's home and office. Continue on to the great big sign, ¼ mile more. Here, winemaker Greg Bruni, who grew up at San Martin Winery, offers an excellent Chardonnay, the first release, and a well-fitted gift shop and deli. Plenty of room for picnicking. The race car collection reflects another investment of this family's construction business fortune.

ESTRELLA RIVER Another 2 miles down Highway 46, on the left, is one of the first wineries established in the area in the 1970s. They have 1,000 acres of grapes, in nine varieties, including the red French Syrah grape, not to be confused with Petite Sirah. Now they also make a sparkling wine.

The nicest way back to town is Union Road. Take Branch Road, the first right beyond Arciero and before Estrella, on Highway 26 East. If you go out to Estrella, you'll have to double back and turn left.

Branch is dirt for about a mile, but it's in pretty good shape, and Union is all paved, through pretty vineyard country. Turn right on Union from Branch. Follow it back to the point where it touches Highway 46.

13

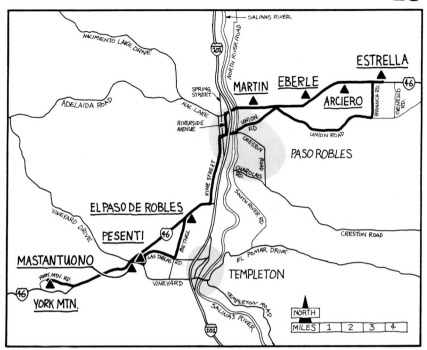

MARTIN Take Highway 46 East to the left, now, the last 1½ miles back to Paso Robles, so you can stop at the new tasting room of this dairy-turned-winery operation. The winery itself is tucked back on Buena Vista Drive. This small, family operation has some interesting varieties, including the Italian Nebbiolo grape, which made Chianti famous.

Return to Paso Robles, crossing the narrow bridge over the Salinas River with care, and turn left onto Riverside Avenue. Follow that back to 13th Street, turn right, pass Spring Street, then turn left onto Vine Street, which is 2 blocks beyond.

You can stop here, or have lunch and continue on in the afternoon for a tour of the wineries south of town.

61

South Vine Street leads south to Highway 46 West. It's another hill climb, but more gradual than the Union Road climb. The wineries start 3 miles out of town.

EL PASO DE ROBLES With a new winery just built at the intersection of Bethel Road, this winery has two couples as its new owners, and the winemaker is Stan Hall, who was with Paul Masson for a decade. Don't miss the Zinfandel.

Two more winery tasting rooms, at the intersection of Vineyard Drive, should be passed if you want to climb up to York Mountain Road and the area's oldest operation.

YORK MOUNTAIN It's 2 miles up to York Mountain Road, and another steep, short climb to the end of that road, but this old winery has loads of charm. Winemaker Steve Goldman and his dad, Max, have maintained the tradition here for 50 years. The winery itself dates from 1882.

MASTANTUONO It's downhill all the way back to Vineyard Drive. The winery on the first corner has the name of its owner, Pasquale Mastantuono, now known as Pat Maston, and his wife, Leona. Boy, have they got Zinfandels!

PESENTI Another old family winery is just to the right, down Vineyard Drive. It's still in the family, which started here in 1923.

Take the left up Winery Road next to Pesenti. It is pretty, quiet country, and the road makes a right onto Las Tablas Road. Follow that to the intersection with Bethel Road. Turn left and follow Bethel to Highway 46. Return to Paso Robles the way you came out, on South Vine Street.

WINERIES TO VISIT

Arciero Winery, Hwy. 46 East (Box 539), Paso Robles 93447. (805) 239-2562. Open daily.

Eberle Winery, Hwy. 46 East (Box 2459), Paso Robles 93447. (805) 238-9607. Open daily.

El Paso de Robles Winery, Hwy. 46 West at Bethel Rd. (Box 548), Paso Robles 93447. (805) 238-6986. Open daily.

Estrella River Winery, Hwy. 46 East (Box 96), Paso Robles 93447. (805) 238-6300. Open daily.

Martin Brothers Winery, Buena Vista Dr., Paso Robles 93446. (805) 238-2520. Tasting room on Hwy. 46 East. Open daily 11–5.

Mastantuono Winery, Hwy. 46 West & Vineyard Dr., Templeton 93465. (805) 238-0676.

Pesenti Winery, 2900 Vineyard Dr., Templeton 93465. (805) 434-1030. Open daily.

York Mountain Winery, York Mountain Rd. West, Rt. 2, Box 191, Templeton 93465. (805) 238-3925. Open daily.

SELECTED STOPS

Paso Robles Chamber of Commerce, 1113 Spring St., Paso Robles 93446. (805) 238-0506.

Paso Robles Inn, 1103 Spring St., Paso Robles 93446. (805) 238-2660.

Bed & Breakfast: Country House Inn, 91 Main St., Templeton 93465. (805) 434-1598.

Roseleith B&B, 1415 Vine St., Paso Robles 93446. (805) 238-5848.

BICYCLE ASSISTANCE: Sunstorm Cyclery, 831 13th St., Paso Robles 93446. (805) 238-4343.

14 San Luis Obispo

WINE RIDES IN A BIKE TOWN

Distance: 19 miles
Terrain: Very mild hills and lovely countryside, with lots of companion bicyclists. Gearing in the 60s.

San Luis is a college town and a bicyclist's paradise—bike routes everywhere, bicycle-aware vehicles, great restaurants, bike parking; in short, you'll wonder why you ever left school.

We stayed at a nice little motel on Monterey Street. There are a number of them. From Monterey, turn left onto California, heading east. This becomes a right onto Johnson and takes you out straight to the wineries, along Orcutt Road.

CHAMISAL This small winery on the right, about 1 mile beyond Biddle Road, specializes in estate-bottled wines made from Norman Goss's plantings, the first ever in Edna Valley. Most of it is Chardonnay. It's always windy here and never too warm, so the wines and the bicycling have a special character.

CORBETT CANYON WINERY About 2 miles down the road is Tiffany Ranch Road, on the right. Turn there, and right again onto Corbett Canyon Road. From this intersection you can see the winery up on the hill. An imposing structure built by Jim Lawrence, it was the first winery in the valley and is happy to receive cyclists.

EDNA VALLEY VINEYARDS The newest winery in this new area is just another few miles up Corbett Canyon after it feeds into Highway 227. On the right is Biddle Road again. Turn right onto Biddle, and the winery is just to the right, again, up on top of the hill. Sleek and efficient, the new winery will also have picnic tables and tasting facilities, but for now it is mostly a working winery. Their production will consist of Chardonnay and Pinot Noir, exclusively. Gary Mosby is the winemaker. His family runs Vega Vineyards, on the next ride.

To return to town, take Highway 227. You'll have plenty of bicycling company and a good shoulder, and time to browse the shops of San Luis before dinner at one of the many nice restaurants.

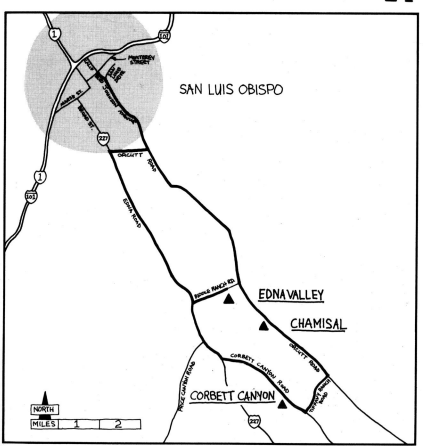

SAN LUIS OBISPO

EDNA VALLEY

CHAMISAL

CORBETT CANYON

NORTH
MILES 1 2

EDNA VALLEY
VINEYARD
1985
Edna Valley
Chardonnay

Estate Bottled

Produced and bottled by
Edna Valley Vineyard
San Luis Obispo, California, USA
Alcohol 13.3 per cent by volume

CORBETT CANYON
VINEYARDS
1986
COASTAL CLASSIC
WHITE ZINFANDEL
from California's Central Coast

WINERIES TO VISIT

Chamisal Vineyard, 7525 Orcutt Rd., San Luis Obispo 93401. (805) 544-3576. Open Wed–Sun, 11–5.

Corbett Canyon Vineyards, 2195 Corbett Canyon Rd., San Luis Obispo 93401. (805) 544-5800. Open daily.

Edna Valley Vineyard, 2585 Biddle Ranch Rd., San Luis Obispo 93401. (805) 544-9594. Open Tues–Sat, 10–4.

SELECTED STOPS

Camping: Lopez Lake Rec. Area, 6800 Lopez Lake Dr., Arroyo Grande 93420. (805) 489-2095.

Pisno State Beach, Hwy. 1. (805) 549-3433.

Bed & Breakfast: Heritage Inn, 978 Olive St., San Luis Obispo 93401. (805) 544-7440.

Madonna Inn, 100 Madonna Rd., San Luis Obispo 93401. (805) 543-3000.

Chamber of Commerce, SLO. (805) 543-1323 (for B&B addresses).

BICYCLE ASSISTANCE: Spirit Cycle Works, 399 Foothill Blvd., San Luis Obispo 93401. (805) 541-5673.

Caution: Some bicyclists here go faster than cars, and silently.

MISSION SAN LUIS

Santa Ynez Valley 15

FROM DENMARK TO THE HIGH COUNTRY

Distance: 15 miles with alternate 12-mile extension.
Terrain: A climb up to the bluff of Solvang, and a short, steep climb to the top of Ballard Canyon Road, but flat, or a long downhill, the rest of the way. Winds in the afternoon out of the southwest.

VEGA Start here, a friendly old ranch home with a handsome new winery and tasting room. The rest rooms are in a big old wine barrel. Take the Santa Rosa Road exit from Highway 101 and go south ½ mile. Park here, and let Jerri and Bill Mosby know you'll be leaving your car for a few hours. Taste their wines on your return.

Follow Santa Rosa Road back towards Highway 101, but continue on beyond your exit to Highway 246, which crosses over Highway 101 and leads to Solvang. Here in Buellton, they say, split pea soup was born.

There is a short pull into Solvang, but the shoulder is wide and the town offers nothing but shops for the visitor. Don't get too distracted, but try the famous Danish pancake with fresh strawberries and cream.

COPENHAGEN This tasting room on Alisal Road, at the far end of Solvang, keeps to the historical theme of this town, while pouring wines under three different labels, including Santa Ynez Valley Winery.

Return to Highway 246 and descend to the stoplight at Alamo Pintado. The mission of Santa Ines is on the right. Turn left at Alamo Pintado, and enjoy the bike lane and more peaceful surroundings.

J. CAREY It's about 2 miles along this flat road to the winery started by the Carey family and now owned by Firestone. The little farmhouse has been converted into an office and tasting room, and don't miss the various years of Cabernet Sauvignon, which reveal what weather and aging can do for a fine wine of this region.

 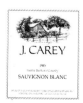 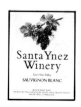 

AUSTEN Continue out Alamo Pintado until it comes to a T at an old clapboard Baptist church. Turn right at the T, and the little town of Los Olivos begins. The winery tasting room is on Grand Avenue, to the left. This perfectly preserved little town is anything but grand, but it's a welcome contrast to the frantic tourist pace of Solvang. Try the Chardonnay.

Return to the T on Alamo Pintado, crossing it to the west this time, as it makes one right angle turn and ends at the beginning of Ballard Canyon Road. There is no street sign, but Ballard Canyon intersects with Highway 154 and becomes Figueroa on the north side. Stay on the south side, climbing a short, steep series of switchbacks up Ballard Canyon, followed by a 3-mile descent back to Highway 246 at Buellton.

Alternate Route

FIRESTONE For an interesting winery but a long uphill climb, instead of taking Ballard Canyon, go west on Highway 154 and in ¼ mile take the right up Foxen Canyon Road. It climbs for about 4 miles, but not a vineyard is in sight until the top. From there it's a steep downhill to the green valley of the Firestone family project. Take the left on Zaca Station Road to the paved winery entrance. Walk over the cattle guards. Built with Firestone tire money, this winery has been thoroughly planned, right down to the grassy courtyard great for a picnic.

It's another mile down to the access to Highway 101. Follow that briefly to Jonata Park Road, which parallels the freeway and becomes Flags Avenue in Buellton, then Santa Rosa Road on the other side of Highway 246.

BALLARD CANYON About 1½ miles down, on the right, turn into this old farm winery. The driveway is full of loose sand, so it will be best to walk the bicycle. Here is another complete tasting room and deli, and oak tree–shaded picnic tables.

Continue down Ballard and expect a few short pulls uphill, but basically it's all downhill to Buellton. Return to Vega, continuing on Santa Rosa Road west another 4 miles for one more winery if you still have the energy.

SANFORD Famous for its fine wines and fine wine label art, this winery is tucked away, and friendly to two-wheeled visitors. Return to Vega for your final tasting.

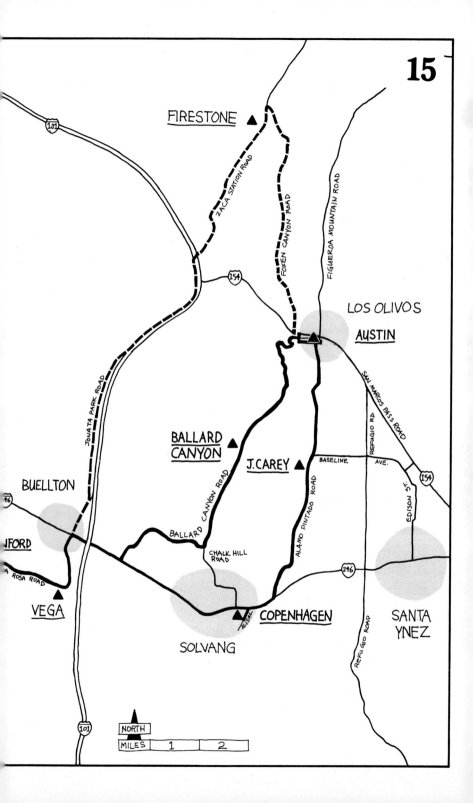

15

15

WINERIES TO VISIT

Austin Cellars, 2923 Grand Ave., Los Olivos 93441. (805) 688-9665.

Ballard Canyon Winery, 1825 Ballard Canyon Rd., Solvang 93463. (805) 688-7585.

J. Carey Cellars, 1711 Alamo Pintado Rd., Solvang 93463. (805) 688-8554.

Copenhagen Cellars, 448 Alisal Rd., Solvang 93463. (805) 688-4218.

The Firestone Vineyard, Zaca Station Rd., Los Olivos 93441. (805) 688-3940. Closed Sundays.

Sanford Winery, 7250 Santa Rosa Rd., Buellton 93427. (805) 688-3300.

Vega Vineyards Winery, Santa Rosa Rd. & Hwy. 101, Buellton 93427. (805) 688-2415.

SELECTED STOPS

Mattei's Tavern, Hwy. 154, Los Olivos 93441. (805) 688-4820.

Camping: Flying Flags Travel Park, Buellton. (805) 688-3716.

Bed & Breakfast: Alisal Guest Ranch, Alisal Rd., Solvang 93463. (805) 688-6411.

Red Rooster Ranch, 2681 Oak Crest Lane, Los Olivos 93441. (805) 688-8050.

Santa Barbara County Vintners, Box WINE, Santa Ynez 93460.

BICYCLE ASSISTANCE: MT Sports, 46 E. Hwy. 246, Buellton 93427. (805) 688-0584.

The Marginal Rider goes international, "God Tur!"

How They Make Wine

Red

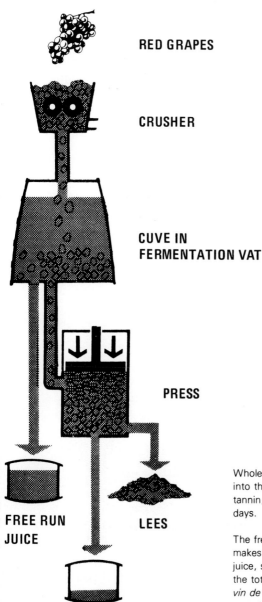

RED GRAPES

CRUSHER

**CUVE IN
FERMENTATION VAT**

PRESS

**FREE RUN
JUICE**

LEES

PRESSED WINE

Whole red grapes are crushed and drop into the *cuve*. The skins give color and tannin, and the must ferments 5 to 13 days.

The free-run juice is siphoned off, and makes the best wine. The remaining juice, skins and seeds (about 4/5ths of the total) pass through the press. The *vin de press* diminishes in quality as it is more heavily extracted from the skins. The lees are used to make alcohol *marc*. Sometimes, the seeds are also pressed to make oil.

How They Make Wine
Rosé

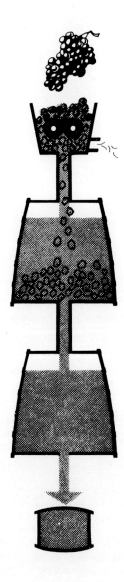

RED GRAPES

FERMENTATION TANK
(Temperature Controlled)

Red grapes are crushed and put into the cuve with skins on, where proper color is achieved, usually within 24 hours.

The skins are removed, and the juice fermented as with white wine.

Temperature control during fermentation gives a fruitier result.

White

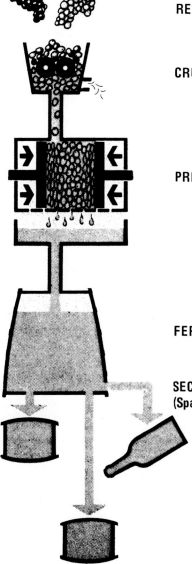

RED OR WHITE GRAPES

CRUSHER

PRESS

FERMENTATION VAT

SECOND FERMENTATION IN THE BOTTLE
(Sparkling Wine)

White grapes and red grapes with white juice are pressed and pass through a gentle, horizontal press, and the juice fermented.

When the natural sugar in the wine has all turned to alcohol, fermentation stops. Sweet wine *vin doux* is removed from the *cuve* before fermentation is complete, leaving some residual sugar. Bubbles are produced *petillant* when the sweet wine is immediately bottled and fermentation finishes in the bottle, creating gas.

CUVE

73

• S U M M E R •

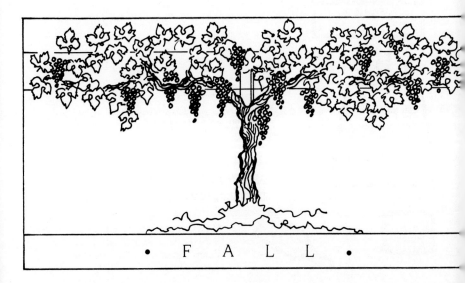

• F A L L •

 "What through youth gave us love and roses, Age still leaves us friends and wine," wrote Thomas Moore.

The Winery Index

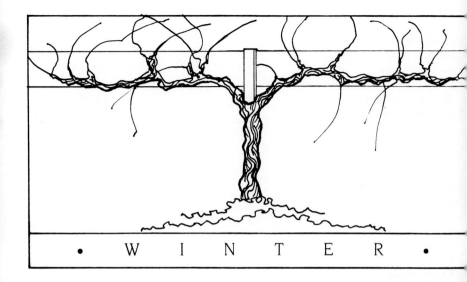

· W I N T E R ·

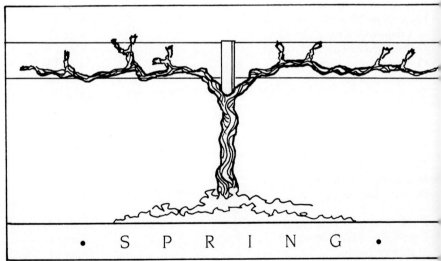

· S P R I N G ·

Permission is granted by Simi Winery.

Illustrations by Mary

"No thing more excellent nor more valuable than wine was ever granted mankind by G
wrote Plato.

The Winery Index (cont.)

The Winery Index (cont.)

Grape Expeditions

The great bicycle guides to the world's wine country.

ORDER FORM

Grape Expeditions in California . . . at **$7.50** ___ copies $ _____
  15 Tours in Napa, Sonoma, Mendocino and the Central and South Coasts

Grape Expeditions in France . . . at **$9.00** ___ copies $ _____
  12 Tours in Loire, Burgundy, Bordeaux, Champagne, the Rhone and Provence

BOTH books for a special price: **$14.50** ___ sets $ _____

  Tax (California residents only) 6% $ _____

  Shipping and handling $ __1.00__

  TOTAL $ _____

[For orders under $20, please enclose payment with order, payable to *Grape Expeditions,* 1442 Willard St., San Francisco CA 94117 USA. Tel. (415) 824-1563.]

Ship to: _____

Address: _____

_____ Zip _____

ORDER FORM

Grape Expeditions in California . . . at **$7.50** ___ copies $ _____
  15 Tours in Napa, Sonoma, Mendocino and the Central and South Coasts

Grape Expeditions in France . . . at **$9.00** ___ copies $ _____
  12 Tours in Loire, Burgundy, Bordeaux, Champagne, the Rhone and Provence

BOTH books for a special price: **$14.50** ___ sets $ _____

  Tax (California residents only) 6% $ _____

  Shipping and handling $ __1.00__

  TOTAL $ _____

[For orders under $20, please enclose payment with order, payable to *Grape Expeditions,* 1442 Willard St., San Francisco CA 94117 USA. Tel. (415) 824-1563.]

Ship to: _____

Address: _____

_____ Zip _____

POSTCARD

TO: Grape Expeditions
1442 Willard Street
San Francisco CA 94117
U.S.A.

(Please use additional paper if needed. We can send gifts.)

POSTCARD

TO: Grape Expeditions
1442 Willard Street
San Francisco CA 94117
U.S.A.

(Please use additional paper if needed. We can send gifts.)